ANIMAL
EXPERIMENTATION

Contemporary Issues

Series Editors: Robert M. Baird
                Stuart E. Rosenbaum

Other titles in this series:

ANIMAL EXPERIMENTATION

THE MORAL ISSUES

EDITED BY

ROBERT M. BAIRD & STUART E. ROSENBAUM

CONTEMPORARY ISSUES

PROMETHEUS BOOKS
AMHERST, NEW YORK

Published 1991 by Prometheus Books

With editorial offices located at 700 East Amherst Street, Buffalo, New York 14215, and distribution facilities at 59 John Glenn Drive, Amherst, New York 14228.

Library of Congress Cataloging-in-Publication Data

Animal experimentation : the moral issues / [edited] by Robert M. Baird and Stuart E. Rosenbaum.
     p.   cm.—(Contemporary issues)
  Includes bibliographical references.
  Summary: Presents articles debating the use of animals in scientific research.
  ISBN 0-87975-667-5 (pap. only)
  1. Animal experimentation—Moral and ethical aspects. 2. Animal rights. [1. Animal experimentation—Moral and ethical aspects. 2. Animals—Treatment—Moral and ethical aspects. 3. Animal rights.] I. Baird, Robert M., 1937-   . II. Rosenbaum, Stuart E. III. Series: Contemporary issues (Buffalo, N.Y.)
HV4915.A64   1991
179'.4—dc20   90-28879
                                              CIP
                                             AC

Printed on acid-free paper in the United States of America

Contents

6 Contents

Introduction

On January 13, 1962, the London *Daily Mirror* ran a story, "The Death of a Hero." The hero was a mongrel dog, Blackie. Blackie, a stray, had ingratiated himself with the Beech family of Manchester several months before the birth of their son, Ian. After Ian was born, Blackie took pleasure in sitting by the pram. When a blazing fire consumed the Beech house, Blackie tried to drag the baby to safety. Blackie failed, and he and Ian died in the fire. The coroner remarked at the inquest that Blackie's teeth marks on Ian's shoulder were "gentle, gripping marks, and not the marks of biting." He added, "We tend to be sentimental about dogs. But I cannot disregard the fact that this dog made an attempt to get the body away from the fire." Ian was found just a foot away from Blackie's outstretched paws.[1]

How ought we to behave toward dogs? Do individual dogs have any claim to our respect, or our consideration, on moral grounds? Does Blackie merit our respect morally? This question is different from the question whether or not we find dogs useful, convenient, companionable creatures that elicit warm feelings or desires to be with and care for them. The question is one of morality: Do we have moral responsibilities toward these creatures of the sort we have toward humans? The likely response to this question by a person arbitrarily chosen from the streets of any Western city is, "Of course we have no real moral responsibilities to them; they are, after all, only animals."

If this arbitrarily chosen person were a Christian, then this remark would likely be accompanied by explanatory comments to the effect that

7

God created the world and its animals ultimately to serve the purposes of people, that "God gave man dominion over" animals. From this perspective, no animals of any kind, no matter how cute, interesting, or convenient they may be, have moral standing. The more tender-minded among these arbitrarily chosen people might temper their talk about dominion over animals with talk about proper stewardship of God's creation, an idea involving responsible use of natural animal resources.

The upshot of this response, tender-minded or not, is that animals have no moral value in themselves and do not in themselves merit moral respect or consideration. Their value is solely instrumental; they have value only as means to human ends. Questions about the proper use of these animal resources are appropriate, but such questions may be answered only in terms of human interests. "Animal interests," whatever they may be, are irrelevant.

Apart from some justification, like the theological explanation, most people would see this likely response to the moral question as inappropriate. Although dogs cannot speak as most persons can, they do have interests and desires, hopes and fears, and pains and pleasures. Although Blackie could not speak, he did have integrity and affection, if not real love, and his loyalty was as remarkable as any human might display. In the face of such apparent facts about dogs and other animals, denying their moral worth seems to indicate moral insensitivity, if not bigotry.

If bigotry is involved, it is of the kind that has come to be known as speciesism. Speciesism is the devaluing of animals simply because they are not human. Apart from some justification for this devaluing of animals, it will likely be seen as morally equivalent to the commonly acknowledged bigotry of racism or sexism, the perspectives that see humans or other races or genders as of less worth simply because they are of other races or genders.

Is there some justification for devaluing nonhuman animals by comparison with humans? Is there an adequate rationale for seeing animals as no more than means to human interests and desires? Advocates of animal liberation or animal rights claim that there is no such justification or rationale. They claim also that some ways of treating animals typically accepted without question in Western societies are morally reprehensible.

The practice of using animals for experimental purposes, the focus of this anthology, is, to most such advocates, a clear symptom of moral bankruptcy. Animal advocates claim that using animals for experimental purposes is as morally repugnant as using Jews, or women, for experimental purposes. The Animal Liberation Front has even carried this moral conviction into action by liberating animals caged in laboratories and destroying equipment used to experiment on them.

To see speciesism in normal experimental practice is to see it as a symptom of the same bigotry we condemn in social symptoms of racism and sexism. As we are justified in rooting out remaining symptoms of racism and sexism, many conclude we are likewise justified in rooting out symptoms of speciesism. The task of rooting out speciesism is much more difficult because, as a culture, we lack awareness of the bigotry in our treatment of animals; our consciousness has not yet been raised about speciesism as it has been raised about racism and sexism. Thus, the Animal Liberation Front feels justified in taking direct action because of what it sees as the moral obtuseness of pervasive attitudes toward animals. As actions against racism and sexism have been significantly successful, so, too, animal liberationists hope, actions against speciesism will eventually achieve the same success.

Jane McCabe expressed another perspective in her *Newsweek* commentary of December 26, 1988. McCabe has a nine-year-old daughter with cystic fibrosis. She asks, "If you had to choose between saving a very cute dog or my equally cute, blonde, brown-eyed daughter, whose life would you choose? It's not a difficult choice is it? My daughter has cystic fibrosis. Her only hope for a normal life is that researchers, some of them using animals, will find a cure. Don't misunderstand. It's not that I don't love animals, it's just that I love Claire more."[2]

Researchers use vast numbers of animals in efforts to defeat diseases like cystic fibrosis, in testing consumer products for toxicity, and in training veterinarians and physicians. Some animals are taken from pounds before they are, as we say euphemistically, "put to sleep" after efforts to locate their owners or find homes for them. Many people think that putting these animals to constructive use in research is preferable to discarding them. Other animals are taken from their natural habitats, while still others are bred specifically for laboratory use. Most such animals, researchers think, are used constructively to make the world a better place for humanity.

Some of these constructive uses of animals inflict significant pain and suffering on them. Research sometimes involves administering drugs in large amounts to find out how well or poorly the animal tolerates them. An example is animal testing of consumer products for toxic effects, usually employing the LD-50 test. This test requires feeding a sufficient quantity of the product in question to find the dose that kills 50 percent of the animals tested. Richard Ryder comments on this test:

> Because most cosmetic products are not especially poisonous, it necessarily follows that if a rat or a dog has to be killed this way, then very great quantities of the cosmetic must be forced into their stomachs, blocking or breaking internal organs, or killing the animal by some other physical action, rather than by any specific chemical effect. Of course the procedure of force-feeding . . . is itself a notoriously unpleasant procedure. . . . When the substance forced into the stomach is not food at all, but large quantities of face powder, makeup or liquid hair dye, then no doubt the suffering is very much greater. If, for the bureaucratic correctness of the test, quantities great enough to kill are involved then clearly the process of dying itself must often be prolonged and agonizing, all the animals being made very ill indeed, half of them just managing to survive, the other half eventually succumbing.[3]

Nevertheless, researchers, along with those who depend for their lives and for the lives of their loved ones on results of research, as well as corporate manufacturers of consumer products, feel strongly that medical progress and consumer safety must not be impeded by overzealous concern for animal welfare. Medical and consumer product research during the twentieth century, involving untold animal suffering, has brought humanity greater control than ever before over the vicissitudes of health and appearance. Now, many who are afflicted with cancer, heart disease, cystic fibrosis, or myriad other ills, can contemplate a future less than bleak; and many who do not measure up to cultural ideals of appearance are able to secure a better life by making use of cosmetic products.

Few would want to sacrifice this greater control, and few are willing to sacrifice the prospect of still greater control in the future. More than a million Americans, and untold millions worldwide, are infected with the AIDS virus. Those infected who have a voice, and the heart for raising it, are demanding greater support from public and private sources for the research necessary to bring this relatively new disease under control. To suggest that respect for animals might be a legitimate barrier to this particular goal would incur the strongest negative reaction from those infected with AIDS. The idea of deliberately sacrificing prospects for greater control of our fates by succumbing to nagging discomfort about how we are treating animals cannot be popular; indeed, it can only be unpopular, and it may even appear morally presumptuous and arrogant.

Still, apart from some explanation, rationale, or justification, using animals as mere instruments to our interests will appear to be a symptom of bigotry. The bigotry, again, is the sort that sees other creatures as of less worth simply because they are not human.

If our use of animals in laboratories is a symptom of simple bigotry, then morally reputable people will exert themselves to stop it. That apparently reputable people not only do not exert themselves to stop laboratory use of animals, but also frequently—as in the case of AIDS research mentioned above—argue in favor of intensifying it, suggests widespread belief that an appropriate explanation, rationale, or justification is readily available. The required explanation will excuse, or rationalize, our use of animals as mere instruments to human interests.

The theological rationale for using animals as mere instruments to human interests is ubiquitous. According to this view, God intended the entire created order for human use; humans have "dominion" over animals and may use them as they see fit for their own benefit. This theological rationale frequently also makes mention of human stewardship over creation, thus conveying the idea of its responsible use. The crux of this idea is that no animal has moral worth or standing in itself because of who it is. There is no "who" for any animal to be. The value of animals is solely what they can contribute to human well-being and flourishing; this contribution is, so to speak, their "highest moral purpose." (Those scare quotes are appropriate because, on this view, animals have no morality, no purpose, and certainly no moral purpose.) Responsible use, according to the stewardship idea, is considerate efficient use, given human needs and desires.

From the perspective of this theological rationale, laboratory use of animals can never become morally disreputable, though questions might be raised about whether or not particular circumstances embody the ideals of good stewardship. Inconsiderate or inefficient use of animals might occasion appropriate criticism, but otherwise this explanation frees human use of animals from moral criticism.

But any explanation, any justification, may be questioned. Just as proponents of unequal treatment for races or genders have seen their justifications questioned, proponents of unequal treatment for species are seeing their justifications questioned. The theological perspective that appeals to biblical authority in support of unequal treatment for races and genders is now widely rejected, much more widely rejected than it was during the nineteenth century. In the matter of voting rights, for example, the fifteenth amendment to the American Constitution, ratified in 1870, and the nineteenth amendment, ratified in 1920, extended them, respectively, to members of all races and both genders, thus ending a kind of unequal treatment previously thought justified. Many people had formerly considered that kind of unequal treatment, along with other kinds now almost universally condemned, justified on theological grounds. In the last decade of the twentieth century, however, few would try to justify racism or sexism on such grounds. Nevertheless, a theological rationale concerning the treatment of animals remains influential in discussions of animal issues. In addition to the "having been given dominion" idea, one finds other appeals to biblical authority. Some will cite God speaking to Noah, following the Flood: "The fear and dread of you will fall upon all the beasts of the earth and all the birds of the air, upon every creature that moves along the ground, and upon all the fish of the sea; they are given into your hands. Everything that lives and moves will be food for you" (Gen. 9: 2–3). The idea that humanity is the apex, the goal, the ultimate development, of the animal kingdom, to which all other life is properly subservient, is common coin, and a literalistic biblical mentality is significantly responsible for it.

Beyond the theological rationale for subjugation of animals to human interests, one finds similar justifications deeply imbedded in Western philosophy. In Aristotle, for example, persons are worthy of moral regard because they are rational animals, and the primary evidence of their rationality is their power of speech; animals, lacking the power of speech, cannot be rational, and hence cannot be worthy of moral regard. In Descartes's view, animals cannot think because they have no power of speech, and because they cannot think they are mere biological machines, soulless sources of behavior-mimicking motion. In Kant's moral theory, persons are enjoined to treat all *rational* beings always as ends and never as means; animals, failing to meet conventional standards of rationality, do not count among those things that must be treated always as ends and never as means. Kant does add that people ought not to treat animals cruelly because they might thereby lose their natural resistance to treating persons cruelly. Once again, animals must not be treated badly, not because of their own worth, but because of possible effects on humans of treating animals badly. This traditional philosophical disposition toward animals is a mirror image of the theological rationale that sees animals as given over to "man's dominion."

The theological rationale for speciesism founders on the same rock that sinks the theological rationale for racism and sexism. The Bible, as much as any other text revered as sacred, is bound to norms and practices of the culture that produced it. If such norms and practices are racist or sexist, responsible people feel morally compelled to reject them, and to reject as well the idea that any text might be authoritative insofar as it commends practices contrary to their own community's most enlightened moral judgments. If the analogy between racism, sexism, and speciesism becomes compelling to responsible people, they will have as little difficulty—so far as the theological rationale for it is concerned—in abandoning speciesism as they have had in abandoning other forms of discriminatory practice.

The philosophical rationale for speciesism, imbedded in Western moral and metaphysical traditions of thought, is harder to sink. Philosophers have thought their moral and metaphysical views are rooted in reason itself and thus have thought that their best intellectual efforts floated ethereally above cultural norms and practices. Consequently, philosophers have not usually considered questioning their own views in the way they have felt entirely comfortable questioning the views of their theologically minded peers. Thus, Peter Singer and Tom Regan, prominent animal advocates whose work is included in this volume, tend to be impatient with the theological rationale, while they tend to be more patient with the philosophical tradition represented by Aristotle, Descartes, and Kant, even though they think the philosophical tradition as badly mistaken as the theological in its conclusions about animals.[4] Indeed, most who deliberate morally about animal issues think of themselves as contending on a neutral battleground above the cultural rocks and water that sustain and sometimes sink theological views; they believe they contend in the ethereal region of reason itself.

Some, though few, who deliberate about these issues are uncomfortable with the idea that philosophical views contend in ethereal regions above the particularities of culture. These thinkers are reluctant to come to the strong conclusions found in most participants on both sides of the animal issues debate; they are reluctant because they think they sense the culturally conditioned character even of views that seem to so many to issue from reason itself. The last essay in this volume, by Alan Freeman and Betty Mensch, expresses this minority view. Their minority perspective, if more widely appreciated, might diminish the number of "absolutists" on both sides of the animal experimentation issue. It would also, perhaps unfortunately, intensify the need for deliberate reflection about the issue, for it yields no clean answers on the question of animal experimentation, no "of course it's all right, they're just animals," and no "absolutely not, under no condition."

The essays that follow appear in five parts. In Part One are four essays we have chosen to introduce the moral controversy about animal experimentation; their style and content will be congenial to readers largely unfamiliar with moral philosophy and will, we believe, motivate further reading and thought about this issue. Part Two contains position statements by two foremost animal advocates, Peter Singer and Tom Regan, along with carefully crafted essays distinctly critical of each of their views. Part Three begins with an essay by Carl Cohen aggressively defending the use of animals in experimental research. Another essay by Edwin Converse Hettinger is a careful critique of Cohen's view, and Peter Harrison's essay creatively defends a neocartesian perspective in denying that animals feel pain. Part Four contains a position statement adopted by the deans of the thirteen medical schools of the Associated Medical Schools of New York, along with two proposals for action to address the condition of animals in experimental facilities. In his essay, "To Do or Not to Do," Peter Singer appears to advocate direct action against experimental facilities, action including not only civil disobedience, but even destruction of the facilities themselves. Bernard Rollin advocates the more moderate course of involving ordinary citizens in making decisions about the justification of particular experimental uses of animals. Part Five contains the concluding essay by Freeman and Mensch challenging important moral and philosophical assumptions on both sides of the issue.

We believe the issue of animal experimentation will present increasingly difficult challenges in the years ahead. Our technological culture will increase pressures for more of the knowledge that can be attained only by the experimental use of animals, and our increasing awareness of what we do to animals in laboratories will yield heightened sensitivity to the pain, agony, and death we inflict on them by our desire for such knowledge. We hope this collection of essays will be a positive contribution to efforts to meet this challenge with some grace and wisdom.

Robert M. Baird
Stuart E. Rosenbaum

NOTES

1. E. Gavin Reeve, "Speciesism and Equality," *Philosophy* 53 (October 1978): 562.

2. Jane McCabe, "Is a Lab Rat's Fate More Poignant than a Child's?" *Newsweek* (26 December 1988): 55.

3. Richard Ryder, *Victims of Science* (London: National Anti-Vivisection Society Limited, 1983), p. 36.

4. Having made this remark, we hasten to balance it by mentioning Regan's anthology, *Animal Sacrifices* (Philadelphia: Temple University Press, 1986), a useful volume that explores the diverse ways various religious traditions regard animals.

Part One

Approaching the Issue

1

Beastly Questions

Robert B. White

We wept and watched, my wife and I, as a little girl fought for her life. She was tiny, frail, helpless, and so very vulnerable. Motionless except as her chest rose and fell spasmodically, there lay Lauren, our first grandchild, born so prematurely that each breath was a desperate and failing effort. We wept, our hearts torn by the growing realization that Lauren might not live. The next day she died. The best care that medicine could offer was not enough. The research on baby lambs and kittens that has given life to many premature infants such as Lauren was still in the future and would come too late for her.

In time, two grandsons, Jonathan and Bryan, were born. Premature babies, they also had to struggle for life. Our pain of uncertainty and of waiting was all to be endured twice again. But the little boys lived. The knowledge gained through research on lambs and kittens gave them life, a gift that Lauren could not have.

The memories of despair and grief at the death of one grandchild and of relief and hope and joy at the life of two others, all of these memories came back to me as I sat at my desk preparing to write this essay in defense of the moral and scientific necessity for the use of animals in medical research. And as I thought of the numerous advances in med-

From *Hastings Center Report* (March/April 1989):39–40. Copyright ©1989 by The Hastings Center. Reprinted by permission of the author and the publisher.

ical care that would have been impossible without experiments on cats and sheep and baby lambs, on dogs and pigs and monkeys and mice, on cows and horses and even armadillos, as I thought of all these advances in medical care that have given health and life to countless people, including my grandsons, my mind was flooded by a host of memories.

First was the memory of an esteemed colleague whose recovery from a near-fatal heart attack was made possible by the use of a newly discovered enzyme that dissolved the clot that fouled his arteries. Later he was restored to nearly perfect health by a coronary arteriogram and a percutaneous transluminal coronary angioplasty. He owes his life to scores of dogs on whom the studies were done to perfect the use of streptokinase, the enzyme that was used to dissolve the clotted blood from his coronary arteries. And he also owes his life to yet other dogs on whom the techniques of coronary arteriography and angioplasty were developed and perfected.

Another colleague whom I recently saw at a medical meeting came next to mind. He had developed disabling arthritis of one hip, but now was able to walk again, thanks to the surgical replacement of his crippled joint. He now walks with a limp, but he walks—only because of dogs that were operated on in the course of research that developed and perfected the artificial hip.

One memory evoked another and then another and then another. I recalled patients who were devastated by poliomyelitis in the terrible epidemic of the 1940s, an epidemic in which one of my closest friends and colleagues contracted the disease and nearly died. He survived miraculously after being confined for many days in a respirator, or, as it was called in those days, an iron lung.

And then came memories from the 1950s when I helped give Salk vaccine to the children in a small town in New England. The little ones howled when I approached them with the syringe and needle. A few years later such children were immunized without screams of fear and pain because by then vaccination against poliomyelitis involved nothing more than sucking on a little cube of sugar containing a few drops of vaccine. In his very moving history of the development of the oral vaccine against poliomyelitis, Albert Sabin gave a graphic description of the thirty years of research that were needed to develop his highly effective vaccine. He made clear that this outstanding contribution to the welfare of mankind would not have been possible without experiments on "many thousands of monkeys and hundreds of chimpanzees."[1] Dr. Sabin's vaccine, since its introduction in 1960, has provided nearly complete protection against poliomyelitis to hundreds of millions of people all over the world. The monkeys and chimps to which he referred have saved thousands of lives and spared hundreds of thousands of children a lifetime marred by paralyzed limbs. Poliomyelitis has been very nearly eradicated throughout the industrialized world and could be eradicated in developing nations if those countries had the resources to do so.

These memories were soon followed by recollection of my experience as a consultant on the burn wards here at my medical school and of the scores of severely burned children and adults whose survival often depended on care perfected through the study of burns experimentally inflicted on pigs and sheep and dogs in the research laboratory. In addition, some of those patients who survived did so because the skin of pigs was used as a temporary graft to cover the raw, oozing areas of their seared flesh.

Then came more recent recollections of my work as a consultant in the care of patients with the acquired immune deficiency syndrome, better known as AIDS. They die slowly and pathetically, these patients with AIDS, and we physicians stand by helplessly as they die because as yet we do not know enough about the virus that causes this dread disease. Thousands are dying from that virus now, and tens of thousands will die in this epidemic in the coming few years unless current research leads to an effective vaccine. This research must include the study of monkeys that are deliberately infected with the AIDS virus. Will the opponents of experimentation on animals prevent present-day researchers from eradicating the AIDS virus, as Dr. Sabin and others, conquered the virus of poliomyelitis?

And finally, I thought of another friend and colleague whose belly was ripped by machine gun fire as he parachuted into Europe during the second world war. Without plasma and blood transfusions, this young medical officer would have died before he could be flown to a hospital in England. If those who oppose the use of animals in medical research had prevailed some fifty years ago, there would have been no research on hemorrhagic shock in dogs. This research cost the life of many dogs that were bled into a state of severe and, at times, fatal shock. But the knowledge gained through the sacrifice of these animals gave medicine the means to save this soldier when he nearly bled to death as he dangled helplessly in his parachute in the French sky in 1944. And there is no counting the number of others, soldiers and civilians, who owe their lives to these experiments on dogs.

And so my memories came, one after the other, but they all led to the same question: "How can any rational, compassionate, and thoughtful person oppose the use of animals in medical research?" Have those who oppose such research watched one grandchild die because of lack of medical knowledge and then, a few years later, watched two other grandchildren be saved by medical procedures that could not have been developed without research on animals? Would they have a young medical officer bleed to death somewhere in war-torn France rather than allow the experiments on dogs that were essential to the development of effective treatment of shock due to massive loss of blood? Are they so blindly opposed to the use of animals in medical research that they would prevent Dr. Sabin's experiments on his "thousands of monkeys and hundreds of chimpanzees" that were necessary to perfect the vaccine that conquered poliomyelitis? Will they tell the thousands of patients who today suffer from AIDS to give up hope because monkeys should not be used in the laboratory in our fight against this plague? Are those who oppose my view on the use of animals in medical research willing to tell my grandsons that it would have been preferable to let them and thousands of other children die rather than allow research on animals? I hope not.

But the fact is, there are people who would let my grandsons die rather than allow any animal to be used in medical research. These are not people who press only for the humane treatment of animals in the laboratory, a cause that no reasonable person can oppose. These are antivivisectionists who will, if they have their way, put a stop to all experimentation on animals no matter the cost to the advancement of health care. The number and the political influence of people in this movement have grown alarmingly in recent years. They have lobbied successfully for a law in Massachusetts to forbid the use of pound animals in biomedical research. And now they are pressing Congress to impose similar restrictions nationwide. If such federal legislation is passed, it will seriously hamper all medical research in this country and will make the cost of some research prohibitively high, as it already has done in Massachusetts.[2]

Those who oppose the use of pound animals in biomedical studies make little or no mention of the fact that only two percent of those animals are used in scientific experiments, while the other ten to fifteen million meet a meaningless and useless death at the pound each year.

And the comments of some of the leaders in the antivivisectionist movement suggest that they are motivated more by personal needs to win a power struggle against the leaders of the biomedical community than by humanitarian concerns for either people or animals. For example, John McArdle, a nationally prominent antivivisectionist, has stated that he believes medical researchers have been placed by the public on a pedestal and he comments: "we're whacking away at the base of that pedestal, and it is going to fall."[3] He also has made the rather macabre suggestion that medical researchers should perform their experiments on brain-dead humans rather than animals. He stated, "It may take people awhile to get used to the idea, but once they do, the savings in animal lives will be substantial."

Another leading antivivisectionist is Ingrid Newkirk, the codirector of PETA, or People for the Ethical Treatment of Animals. She has said that scientists who experiment on animals have been "lying and misleading the public" about the value of research on animals.[4] She stated that the objective of PETA is to attack "the whole grubby system of biomedical research, because if you jeopardize an animal one iota [in doing research] . . . you're doing something immoral. Even painless research is fascism . . ." And, she added, "Animal liberationists do not separate out the human animal, so there is no rational basis for saying that a human being has special rights. A rat is a pig is a dog is a boy."

Jonathan and Bryan, my grandsons, disagree.

NOTES

1. Albert B. Sabin, "Oral Poliovirus Vaccine: History of Its Development and Prospects for Eradication of Poliomyelitis," *Journal of the American Medical Association* 194, no. 8 (1965): 872–76.

2. Katie McCabe, "Who Will Live, Who Will Die," *The Washingtonian* 21, no. 11 (1986): 112–18.

3. Ibid.

4. Ibid.

2

Ethics and Animals

Steven Zak

In December of 1986 members of an "animal-liberation" group called True Friends broke into the Sema, Inc., laboratories in Rockville, Maryland, and took four baby chimpanzees from among the facility's 600 primates. The four animals, part of a group of thirty being used in hepatitis research, had been housed individually in "isolettes"—small stainless-steel chambers with sealed glass doors. A videotape produced by True Friends shows other primates that remained behind. Some sit behind glass on wire floors, staring blankly. One rocks endlessly, banging violently against the side of his cage. Another lies dead on his cage's floor.

The "liberation" action attracted widespread media attention to Sema, which is a contractor for the National Institutes of Health, the federal agency that funds most of the animal research in this country. Subsequently the NIH conducted an investigation into conditions at the lab and concluded that the use of isolettes is justified to prevent the spread of diseases among infected animals. For members of True Friends and other animal-rights groups, however, such a scientific justification is irrelevant to what they see as a moral wrong; these activists remain frustrated over conditions at the laboratory. This conflict between the NIH and animal-rights groups mirrors the tension between animal researchers

From *The Atlantic Monthly* 263, no. 3 (March 1989):69–74. Reprinted in edited form with the permission of the author.

and animal-rights advocates generally. The researchers' position is that their use of animals is necessary to advance human health care and that liberation actions waste precious resources and impede the progress of science and medicine. The animal-rights advocates' position is that animal research is an ethical travesty that justifies extraordinary, and even illegal, measures.

The Sema action is part of a series that numbers some six dozen to date and that began, in 1979, with a raid on the New York University Medical Center, in which members of a group known as the Animal Liberation Front (ALF) took a cat and two guinea pigs. The trend toward civil disobedience is growing. For example, last April members of animal-rights groups demonstrated at research institutions across the country (and in other countries, including Great Britain and Japan), sometimes blocking entrances to them by forming human chains. In the United States more than 130 activists were arrested, for offenses ranging from blocking a doorway and trespassing to burglary.

To judge by everything from talk-show programs to booming membership enrollment in animal-rights groups (U.S. membership in all groups is estimated at 10 million), the American public is increasingly receptive to the animal-rights position. Even some researchers admit that raids by groups like True Friends and the ALF have exposed egregious conditions in particular labs and have been the catalyst for needed reforms in the law. But many members of animal-rights groups feel that the recent reforms do not go nearly far enough. Through dramatic animal-liberation actions and similar tactics, they hope to force what they fear is a complacent public to confront a difficult philosophical issue: whether animals, who are known to have feelings and psychological lives, ought to be treated as mere instruments of science and other human endeavors.

The ALF is probably the most active of the world's underground animal-rights groups. It originated in England, where the animal-protection movement itself began, in 1824, with the founding of the Royal Society for the Prevention of Cruelty to Animals. The ALF evolved from a group called the Bank of Mercy, whose members sabotaged the vehicles of hunters and destroyed guns used on bird shoots. It now has members across Europe, and in Australia, New Zealand, Africa, and Canada, as well as the United States. It does not, however, constitute a unified global network. The American wing of the ALF was formed in 1979. The number of its members is unknown, but their ages range from eighteen to over sixty. Some are students, some are blue-collar workers, and many belong to the suburban middle class.

Animal-rights activists feel acute frustration over a number of issues, including hunting and trapping, the destruction of animals' natural habitats, and the raising of animals for food. But for now the ALF considers animal research the most powerful symbol of human dominion over and exploitation of animals, and it devotes most of its energies to that issue. The public has been ambivalent, sometimes cheering the ALF on, at other times denouncing the group as "hooligans." However one chooses to characterize the ALF, it and other groups like it hold an uncompromising "rights view" of ethics toward animals. The rights view distinguishes the animal-protection movement of today from that of the past and is the source of the movement's radicalism. . . .

Early animal-protection advocates and groups, like the RSPCA, seldom talked about rights. They condemned cruelty—that is, acts that produce or reveal bad character. In early-nineteenth-century England campaigners against the popular sport of bull-baiting argued that it "fostered every bad and barbarous principle of our nature." Modern activists have abandoned the idea that cruelty is demeaning to human character ("virtue thought") in favor of the idea that the lives of animals have intrinsic value ("rights thought"). Rights thought doesn't necessarily preclude the consideration of virtue, but it mandates that the measure of virtue be the foreseeable consequences of others of one's acts.

"Michele" is thirty-five and works in a bank in the East. She has participated in many of the major ALF actions in the United States. One of the missions involved freeing rats, and she is scornful of the idea that rats aren't worth the effort. "That attitude is rather pathetic, really," she says. "These animals feel pain just like dogs, but abusing them doesn't arouse constituents' ire, so they don't get the same consideration. They all have a right to live their lives. Cuteness should not be a factor."

While most people would agree that animals should not be tortured, there is no consensus about animals' right to live (or, more precisely, their right not to be killed). Even if one can argue, as the British cleric Humphrey Primatt did in 1776, that "pain is pain, whether it be inflicted on man or on beast," it is more difficult to argue that the life of, say, a dog is qualitatively the same as that of a human being. To this, many animal-rights activists would say that every morally relevant characteristic that is lacking in all animals (rationality might be one, according to some ways of defining that term) is also lacking in some "marginal" human beings, such as infants, or the senile, or the severely retarded. Therefore, the activists argue, if marginal human beings have the right to live, it is arbitrary to hold that animals do not. Opponents of this point of view often focus on the differences between animals and "normal" human beings, asserting, for instance, that unlike most human adults, animals do not live by moral rules and therefore are not part of the human "moral community."

The credibility of the animal-rights viewpoint, however, need not stand or fall with the "marginal human beings" argument. Lives don't have to be qualitatively the same to be worthy of equal respect. One's perception that another life has value comes as much from an appreciation of its uniqueness as from the recognition that it has characteristics that are shared by one's own life. (Who would compare the life of a whale to that of a marginal human being?) One can imagine that the lives of various kinds of animals differ radically, even as a result of having dissimilar bodies and environments—that being an octopus feels different from being an orangutan or an oriole. The orangutan cannot be redescribed as the octopus minus, or plus, this or that mental characteristic; conceptually, nothing could be added to or taken from the octopus that would make it the equivalent of the oriole. Likewise, animals are not simply rudimentary human beings, God's false steps, made before He finally got it right with us.

Recognizing differences, however, puts one on tentative moral ground. It is easy to argue that likes ought to be treated alike. Differences bring problems: How do we think about things that are unlike? Against what do we measure and evaluate them? What combinations of likeness and difference lead to what sorts of moral consideration? Such problems may seem unmanageable, and yet in a human context we routinely face ones similar in kind if not quite in degree: our ethics must account for dissimilarities between men and women, citizens and aliens, the autonomous and the helpless, the fully developed and the merely potential, such as children or fetuses. We never solve these problems with finality, but we confront them.

One might be tempted to say that the problems are complicated enough without bringing animals into them. There is a certain attractiveness to the idea that animals—lacking membership in the human and moral communities, and unable to reciprocate moral concern—deserve little consideration from us. After all, doesn't one have obligations toward members of one's family and community that do not apply to outsiders? Yet this appeal to a sense of community fails to take into account certain people who likewise lack membership and yet have moral claims against us. Consider future people, particularly those who will live in the distant future. Suppose that our dumping of certain toxic wastes could be predicted to cause widespread cancer among people five hundred years in the future. Would we not have a heavy moral burden to refrain from such dumping? Probably most of us would say that we would. Yet in what meaningful sense can it be said that people we will never meet, who will never do anything for us, and whose cultures and ethical systems will likely be profoundly different from our own, are members of our community? Membership may count for something, but it is clearly not a necessary condition for moral entitlement. Also, some animals—my dog, for instance—may more sensibly be characterized as members of our community than may some human beings, such as those of the distant future.

Both advocates and opponents of animal rights also invoke utilitarianism in support of their points of view. Utilitarianism holds that an act or practice is measured by adding up the good and the bad consequences —classically, pleasure and pain—and seeing which come out ahead. There are those who would exclude animals from moral consideration on the grounds that the benefits of exploiting them outweigh the harm. Ironically, though, it was utilitarianism, first formulated by Jeremy Bentham in the eighteenth century, that brought animals squarely into the realm of moral consideration. If an act or practice has good and bad consequences for animals, then these must be entered into the moral arithmetic. And the calculation must be genuinely disinterested. One may not baldly assert that one's own interests count for more. Animal researchers may truly believe that they are impartially weighing all interests when they conclude that human interests overwhelm those of animals. But a skeptical reader will seldom be persuaded that they are in fact doing so. For instance, a spokesperson for a research institution that was raided by the ALF wrote in the *Los Angeles Times* that we should not be "more concerned with the fate of these few dogs than with the millions of people who are cancer victims." Note the apparent weighing: "few" versus "millions." But her lack of impartiality was soon revealed by this rhetorical question: "Would they [the ALF] really save an animal in exchange for the life of a child?"

Even true utilitarianism is incomplete, though, without taking account of rights. For example, suppose a small group of aboriginal tribespeople were captured and bred for experiments that would benefit millions of other people by, say, resulting in more crash-worthy cars. Would the use of such people be morally acceptable? Surely it would not, and that point illustrates an important function of rights thought: to put limits on what can be done to individuals, even for the good of the many. Rights thought dictates that we cannot kill one rights-holder to save another—or even more than one other—whether or not the life of the former is "different" from that of the latter.

Those who seek to justify the exploitation of animals often claim that it comes down to a choice: kill an animal or allow a human being to die. But this claim is misleading, because a choice so posed has already been made. The very act of considering the taking of life X to save life Y reduces X to the status of a mere instrument. Consider the problem in a purely human context. Imagine that if Joe doesn't get a new kidney he will die. Sam, the only known potential donor with a properly matching kidney, himself has only one kidney and has not consented to give it—and his life—up for Joe. Is there really a choice? If the only way to save Joe is to kill Sam, then we would be unable to do so—and no one would say that we chose Sam over Joe. Such a choice would never even be contemplated.

In another kind of situation there *is* a choice. Imagine that Joe and Sam both need a kidney to survive, but we have only one in our kidney bank. It may be that we should give the kidney to Joe, a member of our community, rather than to Sam, who lives in some distant country (though this is far from clear—maybe flipping a coin would be more fair). Sam (or the loser of the coin flip) could not complain that his rights had been violated, because moral claims to some resource—positive claims —must always be dependent on the availability of that resource. But the right not to be treated as if one were a mere resource or instrument— negative, defensive claims—is most fundamentally what it means to say that one has rights. And this is what members of the ALF have in mind when they declare that animals, like human beings, have rights.

Where, one might wonder, should the line be drawn? Must we treat dragonflies the same as dolphins? Surely not. Distinctions must be made, though to judge definitively which animals must be ruled out as holders of rights may be impossible even in principle. In legal or moral discourse we are virtually never able to draw clear lines. This does not mean that drawing a line anywhere, arbitrarily, is as good as drawing one anywhere else.

The line-drawing metaphor, though, implies classifying entities in a binary way: as either above the line, and so entitled to moral consideration, or not. Binary thinking misses nuances of our moral intuition. Entities without rights may still deserve moral consideration on other grounds: one may think that a dragonfly doesn't quite qualify for rights yet believe that it would be wrong to crush one without good reason. And not all entities with rights need be treated in precisely the same way. This is apparent when one compares animals over whom we have assumed custody with wild animals. The former, I think, have rights to our affirmative aid, while the latter have such rights only in certain circumstances. Similar distinctions can be made among human beings, and also between human beings and particular animals. For example, I recently spent $1,000 on medical care for my dog, and I think he had a right to that care, but I have never given such an amount to a needy person on the street. Rights thought, then, implies neither that moral consideration ought to be extended only to the holders of rights nor that all rights-holders must be treated with a rigid equality. It implies only that rights-holders should never be treated as if they, or their kind, didn't matter. . . .

The question of man's relationship with animals goes back at least to Aristotle, who granted that animals have certain senses—hunger, thirst, a sense of touch—but who held that they lack rationality and therefore as "the lower sort [they] are by nature slaves, and . . . should be under the rule of a master." Seven centuries later Saint Augustine added the authority of the Church, arguing that "Christ himself [teaches] that to refrain from the killing of animals . . . is the height of superstition, for there are no common rights between us and the beasts. . . ." Early in the seventeenth century René Descartes argued that, lacking language, animals cannot have thoughts or souls and thus are machines.

One may be inclined to dismiss such beliefs as archaic oddities, but even today some people act as if animals were unfeeling things. I worked in a research lab for several summers during college, and I remember that it was a natural tendency to lose all empathy with one's animal subjects. My supervisor seemed actually to delight in swinging rats around by their tails and flinging them against a concrete wall as a way of stunning the animals before killing them. Rats and rabbits, to those who injected, weighed, and dissected them, were little different from cultures in a petri dish: they were just things to manipulate and observe. Feelings of what may have been moral revulsion were taken for squeamishness, and for most of my lab mates those feelings subsided with time. . . .

Most states leave the regulation of medical research to Washington. In 1966 Congress passed the Laboratory Animal Welfare Act, whose stated purpose was not only to provide humane care for animals but also to protect the owners of dogs and cats from theft by proscribing the use of stolen animals. (Note the vocabulary of property law; animals have long been legally classified as property.) Congress then passed the Animal

Welfare Act of 1970, which expanded the provisions of the 1966 act to include more species of animals and to regulate more people who handle animals. The AWA was further amended in 1976 and in 1985.

The current version of the AWA mandates that research institutions meet certain minimum requirements for the handling and the housing of animals, and requires the "appropriate" use of pain-killers. But the act does not regulate research or experimentation itself, and allows researchers to withhold anesthetics or tranquilizers "when scientifically necessary." Further, while the act purports to regulate dealers who buy animals at auctions and other markets to sell to laboratories, it does little to protect those animals. For instance, dealers often buy animals at "trade days," or outdoor bazaars of dogs and cats; some people bring cats by the sackful, and, according to one activist, "sometimes you see the blood coming through."

The 1985 amendments to the AWA were an attempt to improve the treatment of animals in laboratories, to improve enforcement, to encourage the consideration of alternative research methods that use fewer or no animals, and to minimize duplication in experiments. . . .

One may believe that virtue thought—which underlies current law —and rights thought should protect animals equally. After all, wouldn't a virtuous person or society respect the interests of animals? But virtue thought allows the law to disregard these interests, because virtue can be measured by at least two yardsticks: by the foreseeable effects of an act on the interests of an animal or by the social utility of the act. The latter standard was applied in a 1983 case in Maryland in which a researcher appealed his conviction for cruelty to animals after he had performed experiments that resulted in monkeys mutilating their hands. Overturning the conviction, the Maryland Court of Appeals wrote that "there are certain normal human activities to which the infliction of pain to an animal is purely incidental"—thus the actor is not a sadist—and that the state legislature had intended for these activities to be exempt from the law protecting animals.

The law, of course, is not monolithic. Some judges have expressed great sympathy for animals. On the whole, though, the law doesn't recognize animal rights. Under the Uniform Commerical Code, for instance, animals—along with refrigerators and can openers—constitute "goods." . . .

Estimates of the number of animals used each year in laboratories in the United States range from 17 million to 100 million: 200,000 dogs, 50,000 cats, 60,000 primates, 1.5 million guinea pigs, hamsters, and rabbits, 200,000 wild animals, thousands of farm animals and birds, and millions of rats and mice. The conditions in general—lack of exercise, isolation from other animals, lengthy confinement in tiny cages—are stressful. Many experiments are painful or produce fear, anxiety, or depression. For instance, in 1987 researchers at the Armed Forces Radiobiology Research Institute reported that nine monkeys were subjected to whole-body irradiation; as a result, within two hours six of the monkeys were vomiting and hypersalivating. In a proposed experiment at the University of Washington pregnant monkeys, kept in isolation, will be infected with the simian AIDS virus; their offspring, infected or not, will be separated from the mothers at birth.

Not all animals in laboratories, of course, are subjects of medical research. In the United States each year some 10 million animals are used in testing products and for other commercial purposes. . . . In 1987, according to the USDA, 130,373 animals were subjected to pain or distress unrelieved by drugs for "the purpose of research or testing." This figure, which represents nearly seven percent of the 1,969,123 animals reported to the USDA that year as having been "used in experimentation," ignores members of species not protected by the AWA (cold-blooded animals, mice, rats, birds, and farm animals). Moreover, there is reason to believe that the USDA's figures are low. For example, according to the USDA, no primates were subjected to distress in the state of Maryland, the home of Sema, in any year from 1980 to 1987, the last year for which data are available.

Steps seemingly favorable to animals have been taken in recent years. In addition to the passage of the 1985 amendments to the AWA, the Public Health Service, which includes the NIH, has revised its "Policy on Humane Care and Use of Laboratory Animals," and new legislation has given legal force to much of this policy. Under the revised policy, institutions receiving NIH or other PHS funds for animal research must have an "institutional animal care and use committee" consisting of at least five members, including one nonscientist and one person not affiliated with the institution.

Many activists are pessimistic about these changes, however. They argue that the NIH has suspended funds at noncompliant research institutions only in response to political pressure, and assert that the suspensions are intended as a token gesture, to help the NIH regain lost credibility. They note that Sema, which continues to keep primates in isolation cages (as regulations permit), is an NIH contractor whose principal investigators are NIH employees. As to the makeup of the animal-care committees, animal-rights advocates say that researchers control who is appointed to them. In the words of one activist, "The brethren get to choose."

However one interprets these changes, much remains the same. For example, the AWA authorizes the USDA to confiscate animals from laboratories not in compliance with regulations, but only if the animal "is no longer required . . . to carry out the research, test or experiment"; the PHS policy mandates pain relief "unless the procedure is justified for scientific reasons." Fundamentally, the underlying attitude that animals may appropriately be used and discarded persists.

If the law is ever to reflect the idea that animals have rights, more drastic steps—such as extending the protection of the Constitution to animals—must be taken. Constitutional protection for animals is not an outlandish proposition. The late U.S. Supreme Court Justice William O. Douglas wrote once, in a dissenting opinion, that the day should come when "all of the forms of life . . . will stand before the court—the pileated woodpecker as well as the coyote and bear, the lemmings as well as the trout in the streams."

Suppose, just suppose, that the AWA were replaced by an animal-rights act, which would prohibit the use by human beings of any animals to their detriment. What would be the effect on medical research, education, and product testing? Microorganisms; tissue, organ, and cell cultures; physical and chemical systems that mimic biological functions; computer programs and mathematical models that simulate biological interactions; epidemiologic data bases; and clinical studies have all been used to reduce the number of animals used in experiments, demonstrations, and tests. A 1988 study by the National Research Council, while finding that researchers lack the means to replace all animals in labs, did conclude that current and prospective alternative techniques could reduce the number of animals—particularly mammals—used in research.

Perhaps the report would have been more optimistic if scientists were as zealous about conducting research to find alternatives as they are about animal research. But we should not be misled by discussions of alternatives into thinking that the issue is merely empirical. It is broader than just whether subject A and procedure X can be replaced by surrogates B and Y. We could undergo a shift in world view: instead of imagining that we have a divine mandate to dominate and make use of everything else in the universe, we could have a sense of belonging to the world and of kinship with the other creatures in it. The us-versus-them thinking that weighs animal suffering against human gain could give way to an appreciation that "us" includes "them." That's an alternative too.

Some researchers may insist that scientists should not be constrained in their quest for knowledge, but this is a romantic notion of scientific freedom that never was and should not be. Science is always constrained, by economic and social priorities and by ethics. Sometimes, paradoxically, it is also freed by these constraints, because a barrier in one direction forces it to cut another path, in an area that might have remained unexplored.

Barriers against the exploitation of animals ought to be erected in the law, because law not only enforces morality but defines it. Until the law protects the interests of animals, the animal-rights movement will by definition be radical. And whether or not one approves of breaking the law to remedy its shortcomings, one can expect such activities to continue. "I believe that you should do for others as you would have done for you," one member of the ALF says. "If you were being used in painful experiments, you'd want someone to come to your rescue."

3

Speciesism

Richard Ryder

Man is just an animal, one species among many species. He is certainly a very clever animal, but he is also an exceptionally destructive, aggressive and polluting animal. During the twentieth century the species of man has grown to overpopulate many areas of the planet and has begun to expand outwards into space, taking with it a potential for creativity as well as the capacity to spoil and to destroy. Man takes with him an advanced technology but only a primitive, intermittent and possibly declining morality. This clever and proud animal has already destroyed many other species; he now also has the power to destroy his own and, as more individuals gain this cataclysmic power, so the probability of total doom for his species grows. Man is, after all, still an animal—he has greater strength than the storm-gods of antiquity but he is still programmed for the jungle.

Whether or not moral schemes are based upon faith, enlightened self-interest or compassion, changes in moral outlook often have been based upon some extension of sympathy so that individuals (such as foreigners, slaves, those of other races) whose rights and interests had not previously been recognized or respected, gain this acknowledgment; they are, as it were, included in the moral in-group. In the nineteenth century the Western world extended its boundaries of compassion to encompass the poor and

From *Victims of Science: The Use of Animals in Research* (London, 1983), pp. 1–8, 11–12, 14.

the enslaved. In some cases this increase in respect for the interests of others genuinely was based upon principle and compassion—it was not because of self-interest but in spite of it.

The first part of the twentieth century has seen the continuation of this trend with an increased recognition by the powerful races of the interests of the weaker ones. The time has now come to extend the borders of respect still further to include a concern for the sufferings of species other than our own.

It was in 1859 that Charles Darwin first published *The Origin of Species,* but it has taken time for its message of evolutionary kinship between man and beast to sink in and be acted upon. Most men intellectually accept their biological relationship with other animals without taking the logical step of acknowledging a *moral* relationship, that is to say treating animals as what they really are—our relatives.

If we examine the arguments used by slave owners in the past to counter those of the reformers, we can see a striking similarity with the view expressed today by those who defend the exploitation of animals in factory-farms, the fur-trade, laboratories and elsewhere. The slave-owners discouraged travelers' visits to the plantations because they considered that such visitors were not experts and therefore tended to react emotionally to what they saw, not understanding, so it was said, the high-mindedness of such ventures nor the technical problems involved. It might be conceded that there were "isolated" whippings and the mortality rate was rather high, but the average slaver could assure his "ill-informed" or "over-sensitive" visitor that he felt a deep compassion for his slaves and they reciprocated this with loyalty and devotion. After all, their living conditions were much better than in the jungle and, besides, these creatures had never known sophisticated pleasures and so what they did not know about they could not miss. The visitor must not judge slaves by his own standards—to believe that they could feel and suffer in a way similar to himself was to be merely "sentimental." Above all else, it would be stressed, slavery was necessary for economic survival.

Such arguments thrive to this very day in the mouths of those who have an interest in the exploitation of animals, although scientists should know better, for they often base the whole validity of biology on the assumption that man is indeed an animal like other animals, and that the study of animals will produce knowledge applicable to man. They cannot have it both ways; either men and animals are entirely different, in which case much of their work is invalid, or else men and the other animals are rather the same, in which case animals logically deserve similar treatment and consideration.

There is hardly a scientist alive today who does not accept the basic Darwinian assertion that men and animals are on the same biological continuum. What reason can there be, other than a sentimental one, for not putting men and animals upon the same *moral* continuum?

For too long man has arrogantly exaggerated his uniqueness. Anthropologists differ in their opinions but many have labeled the great beetle-browed Neanderthal Man as being of a different species from modern man, and not even our linear ancestor. Nevertheless, this entirely different and now extinct creature practiced ritual burial and had a brain larger than our own. It is therefore important to realize that it is not only modern *homo sapiens* who has been capable of displaying great intelligence— at least one other creature of the past demonstrates that man has had no monopoly on abstract thought. We may even be underestimating the intelligence and the cultures of other species extant today.

Some physical differences between species do, of course, exist. But science itself has produced progressively more evidence to suggest that major differences between men and the other animals are less than were once imagined; man now knows he is not the only toolmaker, he does not have the largest or heaviest brain or the largest brain-to-body ratio, he is not the only species with a language, and although he cannot communicate in another animal's symbols, chimpanzees have learned to communicate in his own, inventing new and meaningful combinations of words in American Sign Language for the Deaf (see *Animals, Men and Morals,* p. 79). In some environments man is not the best adapted species and in some special instances not the most intelligent. Certainly man is, on average, very clever, but he took thousands of years to develop his technology beyond the level of the simple stone-axe, and in some parts of the planet this development has only taken place within this century. Many of his apparent advantages over the other creatures depend upon his relatively recent discovery of how to pass on knowledge to future generations; but men isolated from civilization, illiterate and reared in total ignorance of technology, would probably survive, if at all, no better than other animals, practically tool-less and speechless for generations, without the discovery of fire or the luxuries of agriculture.

But how can such differences as exist affect the moral case? Can it seriously be argued that because man is cleverer than other animals he therefore has rights or interests that other animals do not have? Surely, a superior understanding entails greater responsibility rather than the opposite; just as an adult recognizes a degree of responsibility towards an infant, so also should he towards animals. There seems no good reason why physical differences *between* species should affect such matters differently than do physical differences *within* species; there exist many individuals of the human species who, on account of injury to their brains or because of congenital dysfunctions are, permanently or temporarily, less intelligent, less communicative and less able to stand up for themselves than the average dog, cat or monkey. Yet, if a scientist presumed to experiment upon them, to poison them or electrocute them or inject them with diseases, he would rightly stand condemned. Similarly, many adult animals surely possess all the faculties, and more than those, of the human infant—but this does not justify experiments on babies.

All such physical differences are morally irrelevant. To be cruel to a weak creature but not to a strong one is the morality of the coward and the bully. If some creatures from outer space invaded Earth and proved to be stronger or vastly more intelligent than ourselves, would they be justified in ordering us to be vivisected? They might explain to us that, after all, they were very much more intelligent, that they doubted whether we really could feel pain, that they would keep us in perfectly clean and hygienic cages and that they naturally regretted having to perform severe experiments upon us but that it was, unfortunately, necessary for the benefit of their own species. One can imagine one of their scientists trying to justify himself in these terms—"Please don't think I am a sadist. As a matter of fact I am very fond of humans and keep several as pets. I can assure you that I would be the first to criticize any experiments that were unnecessary or involved unnecessary cruelty. I agree that fifty million humans die in our laboratories every Earth-year, but most of these are in routine experiments that do not involve severe pain. You really must not allow your emotions to cloud the issue."

The most important qualities that men share with the other animals are life and sentience. There is as much evidence to believe that another animal can suffer as there is to believe that another individual of one's own species can suffer. There is good evidence that pain is a function of the nervous system and that many animals have nervous systems very much like our own—so, is it not reasonable to assume that when a wounded animal screams and struggles that it is suffering in a way similar to that in which a wounded man can suffer? The capacity to suffer is the crucial similarity between men and animals that binds us all together and places us all in a similar moral category. Those politicians who still believe that politics has some remote connection with morality or who vaguely believe that their job has to do with increasing the total sum of happiness, should question why non-human animals should not be also represented by them? After all, the fully democratic politician already represents the interest of human citizens who do not vote—children, lunatics and lords—so why not also animals? Why should the animals in a state or a constituency or a country not also be accorded some status as citizens? The important question about animals, as Jeremy Bentham pointed out, is not "Can they *reason?* nor can they *talk?* but, can they *suffer?*"

It used to be said that what distinguishes the species from each other is that they cannot interbreed; indeed such was once the core of the definition of "species." But this is no longer regarded as true, for lions and tigers, as an example, are known to be able to interbreed and produce viable hybrids which are themselves capable of reproduction; and yet lions and tigers are still classified as being of separate species. Man is zoologically placed in the so-called Primate Order along with all the species of monkeys and apes, and although there are no well-authenticated accounts of man successfully interbreeding with any other species of primate, the possibility that this could happen still, at least theoretically, remains. Such an event would cause a bureaucratic upheaval! Would the ape-man offspring be accorded all the rights of a citizen in the welfare state? Would the monkey mother receive maternity payments and free health benefits, would the child legally be obliged to attend school at a certain age and receive the right to vote when majority is reached? If this ever occured the moral and legal reassessments provoked by the happy event would be greater than the zoological surprise, because many cases of interbreeding between primate species have already been recorded; undoubtedly, however, it would highlight the absurdity of mankind's current species-centered morality.

In recent decades the word "species" has taken on almost magical undertones and many laymen seem to imagine that the zoologists can always draw some hard and fast line between the species which somehow might justify not only scientific but also moral discriminations. This is not the case and there is in fact no single criterion which distinguishes between all so-called species. Labels such as "race," "sub-species" and "breed" still form the substance of controversies. To make matters even more confusing, there are even groups of animals which are reckoned to be of the *same* species but which apparently *cannot* interbreed.

I use the word "speciesism" to describe the widespread discrimination that is practiced by man against the other species, and to draw a parallel with racism. Speciesism and racism are both forms of prejudice that are based upon appearances—if the other individual looks different then he is rated as being beyond the moral pale. Racism is today condemned by most intelligent and compassionate people and it seems only logical that such people should extend their concern for other races to other species also. Speciesism and racism (and indeed sexism) overlook or underestimate the similarities between the discriminator and those discriminated against and both forms of prejudice show a selfish disregard for the interests of others, and for their sufferings.

Speciesism denies the logic of Evolution. Indeed, the Oxford zoologist Richard Dawkins attacks the prejudice of speciesism on biological grounds (*The Selfish Gene,* Oxford University Press, 1976):

Many of us shrink from judicial execution of even the most horrible human criminals, while we cheerfully countenance the shooting without trial of fairly mild animal pests. Indeed we kill members of other harmless species as a means of recreation and amusement. A human fetus, with no more human feeling than an ameba, enjoys a reverence and legal protection far in excess of those granted to an adult chimpanzee. Yet the chimp feels and thinks and—according to recent experimental evidence—may even be capable of learning a form of human language. The fetus belongs to our own species, and is instantly accorded special privileges and rights because of it. Whether the ethic of "speciesism," to use Richard Ryder's term, can be put on a logical footing any more sound than that of "racism" I do not know. What I do know is that it has no proper basis in evolutionary biology.

. . . The main speciesist defense of cruelty to animals is that mankind benefits—in terms of knowledge, economy or sport, for example. [This] defense of the exploitation of animals in laboratories usually takes the form of arguing that knowledge gained from such research will be of benefit to the human species. But such indeed was the argument put forward by some of the Nazi scientists tried for their experiments upon Jews, and with some scientific justification, for research upon human beings is more likely to produce results beneficial to humans than is research upon other animals.

I believe the speciesist case for animal experimentation is not acceptable. In the first place a large amount of the research which is done is trivial and the knowledge gained has no medical importance. . . . Furthermore, a very great deal of research is after pure knowledge and there is no application for this knowledge in mind at the time of the experimentation. Knowledge, however important or practical it may seem, is itself essentially a *neutral* thing. Science gives men power to act destructively as well as constructively. Knowledge is not always good as Adam and Eve are alleged to have discovered, and as thousands of inhabitants of Nagasaki and Hiroshima also learned. Knowledge about radiation, for example, can be used for the treatment of illness or for the destruction of life. Even new strictly medical knowledge can be, and is, evilly applied to torture (*New Scientist*, 15 November 1973, p. 459), brainwash, extort, change, persuade, punish or annihilate, if it falls into the hands of the wrong people.

Those with genuinely humane motives are most likely to prolong life or alleviate suffering by bringing existing medical knowledge to bear in those parts of the world where men and women are suffering and dying because they cannot afford treatment. Yet many scientists prefer to spend their lives in laboratories causing untold suffering to animals in questionable medical research with a strong commercial motive; these researchers are not convincing when they plead that humanity is their overriding concern.

It cannot be denied that out of all the millions of experiments performed upon animals, some useful knowledge has been gained. But equally it must not be forgotten that this knowledge often could have been acquired by other means and that many of the greatest discoveries of all have owed nothing to the use of laboratory animals and indeed might have been lost if animals had been used.

To impose suffering, allegedly in order to reduce it, and to take life, allegedly in order to save it, are self-contradicting claims. They are made even more dubious when one bears in mind that at the time of the experiment any benefits that might be accrued from it are merely hypothetical and uncertain. To attempt to justify the *certain* suffering of animals against some future, as yet *uncertain* benefit, seems to be an unwarranted gamble. Furthermore, the suffering imposed upon a laboratory animal is quite deliberate and *artificial,* in the sense that if the experiment was not performed then the suffering would not occur; but the suffering that it is hoped to reduce by doing the experiment is caused either by *natural* illness or by *self-inflicted* risks (e.g., through the use of a new cosmetic)—in other words the speciesist attempts to justify the deliberate infliction of suffering upon an innocent animal by claiming that the knowledge so obtained may perhaps, somewhere at some unknown moment in the future, relieve the natural or self-inflicted pains of his own species. This seems to be an entirely selfish, prejudiced and logically unsound argument. . . .

Speciesism is as great a prejudice as racism. Those of us who count ourselves as Socialists or Liberals, Humanitarians or Christians, should extend our ideologies to include the other species; the welfare of animal-citizens should be as much our concern as is that of other humans.

I believe our respect for others should include all sentients. To continue to exclude them from our morality is to be guilty of speciesism. If we accept that it is wrong to cause suffering to innocent humans then, logically, it is also wrong to do this to non-humans. There is no sound evidence for believing that other animals cannot suffer like ourselves, and indeed the evidence points the other way.

For these reasons I consider that animal welfare is a serious subject worthy of further research and deserving the support of governments and the respect of the community in an age when animals increasingly are being exploited.

The next great step forward in Man's moral evolution will be the full recognition of the rights and interests of the animal kingdom.

4

Are Animals People Too?

Robert Wright

I recently interviewed several animal rights activists in hopes that they would say some amusing, crazy-sounding things that might liven up this article. More often than not I was disappointed. They would come close to making unreservedly extremist pronouncements but then step back from the brink, leaving me with a quote that was merely provocative. For example, Ingrid Newkirk, cofounder of People for the Ethical Treatment of Animals (PETA), seemed on the verge of conceding that Frank Perdue is no better than Adolf Hitler—a proposition that technically follows from her premise that animals possess the moral status of humans (and from references in animal rights literature to the ongoing "animal holocaust"). But she wouldn't go all the way. "He's the animals' Hitler, I'll give you that," she said. "If you were a chicken . . . you wouldn't think he was Mother Teresa." The other cofounder of PETA, Alex Pacheco, was not much more helpful. "You and I are equal to the lobsters when it comes to being boiled alive," he said, raising my hopes. But, he added, "I don't mean I couldn't decide which one to throw in, myself or the lobster."

The biggest disappointment was a woman who went by the pseudonym "Helen." She was a member of the Animal Liberation Front, a shadowy group that goes around breaking into scientific laboratories, documenting the conditions therein, and sometimes burning down the labs (minus the animals, which are typically "liberated"—taken somewhere else—in the process). Given all the intrigue involved in interviewing "Helen"—I had to "put out the word" that I wanted to talk with an ALF member, and when she called she always used a streetside phone booth and never left a number—I expected a rich encounter. This hope grew when I found out that she had participated in a recent lab-burning at the University of Arizona. But as professed arsonists go, Helen seemed like a very nice and fairly reasonable person. She was a combination of earnest moral anguish ("For the most part, people just aren't aware of how much suffering and death goes into what they eat and wear. . . . Most people just literally don't know") and crisp professionalism ("Whether I have any animosity toward [laboratory researchers] is irrelevant. . . . I just do everything I can to move them into a different job category"). And though her reverence for life may strike you as creepy—she picks up spiders off the floor and moves them outdoors, rather than squash them—it is not unbounded. She assured me that if termites were destroying her home, she would call an exterminator.

One reason for this general failure to gather satisfactorily extremist quotes is that animal rights activists have become more media-savvy, developing a surer sense for when they are being baited. But another reason is my own failure to find their ideas extremist. Slowly I seem to be getting drawn into the logic of animal rights. I still eat meat, wear a leather belt, and support the use of animals in important scientific research. But not without a certain amount of cognitive dissonance.

The animal rights movement, which has mushroomed during the past decade, most conspicuously in the growth of PETA (membership around 300,000), is distinguished from the animal welfare movement, as represented by, for example, the Humane Society of the United States. Animal *welfare* activists don't necessarily claim that animals are the moral equivalent of humans, just that animals' feelings deserve some consideration; we shouldn't needlessly hurt them—with pointless experimentation, say, or by making fur coats. And just about every thinking person, if pressed, will agree that animal welfare is a legitimate idea. Hardly anyone believes in kicking dogs.

But the truth is that animal welfare is just the top of a slippery slope that leads to animal rights. Once you buy the premise that animals can experience pain and pleasure, and that their welfare therefore deserves *some* consideration, you're on the road to comparing yourself with a lobster. There may be some exit ramps along the way—plausible places to separate welfare from rights—but I can't find any. And if you don't manage to find one, you wind up not only with a rather more sanguine view of animal rights but also with a more cynical view of the concept of human rights and its historical evolution.

None of this is to say that a few minutes of philosophical reflection will lead you to start wearing dumpling-shaped fake-leather shoes, sporting a "Meat is Murder" button, or referring to your pet dog as your "companion animal." The stereotype about the people who do these things— that they're ill at ease in human society, even downright antagonistic toward other humans—is generally wrong, but the stereotype that they're, well, *different* from most people is not. These are dyed-in-the-wool activists, and if they weren't throwing themselves into this cause, they would probably be throwing themselves into some other cause. (Pacheco, for example, had originally planned to become a priest.) Moreover, very few of them were converted to the movement solely or mainly via philosophy. Many will say they were critically influenced by the book *Animal Liberation* (1975), written by the Australian ethicist Peter Singer, but reading Singer was for most of them merely a ratifying experience, a seal of philosophical approval for their intuitive revulsion at animal suffering. Pacheco received a copy of the book the same week he got grossed out while touring a Canadian slaughterhouse. He later gave a copy to Newkirk, who was then chief of Animal Disease Control for the District of Columbia. Around that time she spent a day trying to rescue some starving, neglected horses that were locked in their stalls and mired in mud. That's when it hit her: "It didn't make sense. I had spent the whole day trying to get some starving horses out of a stall and here I was going home to eat some other animal." This gut perception is a recurring theme, as crystallized by Helen: "I just realized that if I wouldn't eat my dog, why should I eat a cow?"

Good question. And implicit in it is the core of the case for animal rights: the modest claim—not disputed by anyone who has ever owned a dog or cat, so far as I know—that animals are sentient beings, capable of pleasure and pain. People who would confine natural rights to humans commonly talk about the things we have that animals don't—complex language, sophisticated reasoning, a highly evolved culture. But none of these is important, for moral purposes, in the way that sheer sentience is.

One way to appreciate this is through a simple thought experiment. Suppose there's a planet populated by organisms that look and act exactly like humans. They walk, talk, flirt, go to law school, blush in response to embarrassing comments, and discuss their impending deaths in glum tones. Now suppose it turns out they're automatons, made out of silicon chips—or even made out of flesh and blood. The important thing is that all their behavior—their blushing, their discussion of death—is entirely a product of the physical circuitry inside their heads and isn't accompanied by any subjective experience; they can't feel pain, pleasure, or anything else. In other words (to use the terminology of Thomas Nagel), it isn't like anything to be them.

Is there anything particularly immoral about slapping one of them in the face? Most everyone would say: obviously not, since it doesn't hurt. How about killing one of them? Again, no; their death doesn't preclude their future experience of happiness, as with real live humans, or cause any pain for friends and relatives. There is no apparent reason to bestow any moral status whatsoever on these creatures, much less the exalted status that the human species now enjoys. They have powerful brains, complex language, and high culture, but none of this makes them significant.

Now rearrange the variables: subtract all these attributes and add sentience. In other words, take all the robots off the planet and populate it with non-human animals: chimps, armadillos, dogs, etc. Is there anything immoral about gratuitously hurting or killing one of these? Do they have individual rights? Most people would answer yes to the first question, and some would answer yes to the second. But the main point is that few people would quickly and easily say "no" to either, because these are harder questions than the robot question. Sentience lies at the core of our moral thinking, and language, intelligence, etc., lie nearer the periphery. Sentience seems definitely a necessary and arguably a sufficient condition for the possession of high moral status (experiments 1 and 2, respectively), whereas the other attributes are arguably necessary but definitely not sufficient (experiments 2 and 1, respectively).

The best way to get a better fix on exactly which traits are prerequisites for moral status is simply to try to explain why they *should* be. Take sentience first. We all agree from personal experience that pain is a bad thing, that no one should have the right to inflict it on us, and consistency (part of any moral system) dictates that we agree not to inflict it on anyone else. Makes sense. But now try to say something comparably compelling about why great reasoning ability or complex language are crucial to moral status. Also, try to do the same with self-consciousness—our awareness of our own existence. (This is another uniquely human attribute commonly invoked in these discussions, but we couldn't isolate it in experiment 1 above because an organism can't have it without having sentience.)

If you accept this challenge, you'll almost certainly go down one of two paths, neither of which will get you very far. First, you may try to establish that self-consciousness, complex language, etc., are the hallmarks of "spirit," the possession of which places us in some special category. This is a perfectly fine thing to believe, but it's hard to *argue* for. It depends much more on religious conviction than on any plausible line of reasoning.

The second path people take in asserting the moral significance of uniquely human attributes is even less successful, because it leads to a booby trap. This is the argument that self-consciousness and reason and language give humans a dimension of suffering that mere animals lack: because we can anticipate pain and death; and because we know that death will represent the end of our consciousness forever; and because we recognize that threats to one citizen may represent a threat to us all—because of all this, the protection of human rights is essential to everyone's peace of mind; the torture or murder of anyone in town, as conveyed to the public via language and then reflected upon at length, makes everyone tremendously fearful. So a robust conception of individual rights is essential for the welfare of a human society in a way that it isn't for, say, the welfare of a chicken society.

Sounds nice, but it amounts to philosophical surrender. To rely completely on this argument is to concede that language, reason, and self-consciousness are morally important *only* to the extent that they magnify suffering or happiness. Pain and pleasure, in other words, are the currency of moral assessment. The several uniquely human attributes may revaluate the currency, but the currency possesses some value with or without them. And many, if not all, non-human animals seem to possess the currency in some quantity. So unless you can come up with a non-arbitrary reason for saying that their particular quantities are worthless while our particular quantities are precious, you have to start thinking about animals in a whole new light. This explains why Peter Singer, in *Animal Liberation*, readily admits that the human brain is unique in its ability to thus compound suffering.

Once the jaws of this philosophical trap have closed on the opponents of animal rights, no amount of struggling can free them. Let them insist that language, reason, and self-consciousness *immensely* raise the moral stakes for humans. Let them add, even, that our sheer neurological complexity makes us experience raw pain more profoundly than, say, dogs or even mice do. Grant them, in other words, that in the grand utilitarian calculus, one day of solid suffering by a single human equals one day's suffering by 10,000 laboratory rats. Grant them all of this, and they still lose, because the point is that animals have now been *admitted* to the utilitarian calculus. If it is immoral, as we all believe it is, to walk up to a stranger and inflict 1/10,000 of one day's suffering (nine seconds' worth), then it is equally immoral to walk up and inflict one day's suffering on a single laboratory rat.

Actually, granting animals utilitarian value doesn't technically mean you have to extend individual rights to them. As far as sheer philosophical consistency goes, you can equally well take rights away from humans. You can say: sure, it makes sense to kill 100 baboons to save the life of one human, but it also makes sense to kill a human to save the life of 100 baboons. Whatever you say, though, you have to go one way or the other, letting such equations work either in both directions or in neither. Unless you can create a moral ratchet called "human rights"—and I don't see any way to do it—you have to choose between a planet on which every sentient creature has rights and a planet on which none does.

And of course if no creature on earth has rights, then it can make sense to kill a human not just for the sake of 100 baboons, but for the sake of two humans—or just in the name of the greater good. In other words, the logic used by animal rights activists turns out to play into the hands of the Adolf Hitlers of the world no less than the Albert Schweitzers. In *Darkness of Noon,* when Ivanov describes Stalin's rule as belonging to the school of "vivisection morality," Arthur Koestler is onto something more than good allegory.

Before figuring out whether to follow this logic toward vegetarianism or totalitarianism, let's remove it from the realm of abstraction. Spending an evening watching videotapes supplied by PETA—such as *The Animals Film,* narrated by Julie Christie—is a fairly disturbing experience. This is partly because the people who made it gave it a subtle shrillness that reflects what is most annoying about the animal rights movement. There are man-on-the-street interviews conducted by an obnoxious, self-righteous interrogator demanding to know how people can own dogs and eat Big Macs; there is the assumption that viewers will find the late McDonald's founder Ray Kroc—a seemingly likeable guy shown innocently discussing how he settled on the name "McDonald's"—abhorrent; there is a simple-minded anticapitalist undercurrent (as if factory farmers in socialist countries spent their time giving foot massages to hogs); and there is grating atonal music meant to make the sight of blood more disturbing than it naturally is.

And that's plenty disturbing, thank you. Take, for example, the chickens hung by their feet from a conveyer belt that escorts them through an automatic throat slicing machine—this the culmination of a life spent on the poultry equivalent of a New York subway platform at rush hour. Or consider the deep basketfuls of male chicks, struggling not to smother before they're ground into animal feed. There's also, naturally, the veal: a calf raised in a crate so small that it can't even turn around, much less walk—the better to keep the flesh tender. There are wild furry animals cut almost in half by steel-jawed traps but still conscious. There are rabbits getting noxious chemicals sprayed in their eyes by cosmetics companies.

And these are the animals that *don't* remind you of human beings. Watching these portions of *The Animals Film* is a day at the zoo compared with watching non-human primates suffer. If you don't already have a strong sense of identity with chimpanzees, gorillas, and the like—if you doubt that they're capable of crude reasoning, anticipating pain, feeling and expressing deep affection for one another—I suggest you patronize your local zoo (or prison, as animal rights activists would have it) and then get hold of a copy of the ethologist Frans de Waal's two amazing books, *Peacemaking Among Primates* and *Chimpanzee Politics*. The commonly cited fact that chimps share about ninety-eight percent of our genes is misleading, to be sure; a handful of genes affecting the brain's development can make a world of difference. Still, if you can watch a toddler chimp or gorilla for long without wanting to file for adoption, you should seek professional help.

In videotapes that Helen helped steal in 1984 from the University of Pennsylvania's Head Injury Clinical Research Center, anesthetized baboons are strapped down and their heads placed in boxlike vices that are violently snapped sixty degrees sideways by a hydraulic machine. Some of the baboons have what appear to be seizures, some go limp, and none looks very happy. Some of the lab workers—as callous as you'd have to become to do their job, perhaps—stand around and make jokes about it all. It's hard to say how much scientific good came of this, because the scientist in question refuses to talk about it. But watching the tapes, you have to hope that the data were markedly more valuable than what's already available from the study of injured humans. In any event, the experiments were halted after PETA publicized the tapes (though ostensibly for sloppy lab technique, such as occasionally inadequate anesthesia, not because of the violent nature of the experiments).

There are certainly many kinds of animal research that seem justified by any reasonable utilitarian calculus. A case in point is the lab Helen helped set afire at the University of Arizona. Among the researchers whose work was destroyed in the attack is a man named Charles Sterling, who is studying a parasite that causes diarrhea in both animals and humans and kills many children in the Third World every year. There is no way fruitfully to study this parasite in, say, a cell culture, so he uses mice, infecting them with the parasite and thereby inducing a non-lethal spell of diarrhea. (The idea repeated mindlessly by so many animal rights activists—that there's almost always an equally effective non-animal approach to experimentation—is wrong.)

Sterling is one of a handful of workers in this area, and he figures, in over-the-phone, off-the-cuff calculations, that all together they cause around 10,000 to 20,000 mice weeks of diarrheal discomfort every year. The apparently realistic goal is to find a cure for a disease that kills more than 100,000 children a year. Sounds like a good deal to me. Again, though, the hitch is that to endorse this in a philosophically impeccable way, you have to let go of the concept of human rights, at least as classically conceived.

Then again, human rights isn't what it's classically conceived as being. It isn't some divine law imparted to us from above, or some Platonic truth apprehended through the gift of reason. The idea of individual rights is simply a non-aggression pact among everyone who subscribes to it. It's a deal struck for mutual convenience.

And, actually, it's in some sense a very old deal. A few million years ago, back when human ancestors were not much smarter than chimps, they presumably abided by an implicit and crude concept of individual rights, just as chimps do. Which is to say: life within a troop of, say, fifty or sixty individuals was in practical terms sacred. (Sure, chimps occasionally murder fellow troop members, just as humans do, but this is highly aberrant behavior. Rituals that keep bluster and small-scale aggression from escalating to fatality are well-developed. And when they fail, and death occurs, an entire chimp colony may be solemn and subdued for hours or longer as if in mourning.) At the same time, these prehuman primates were presumably much like chimps in being fairly disdainful of the lives of fellow species-members who didn't belong to the troop. At some point in human history, as troops of fifty became tribes of thousands, the circle of morally protected life grew commensurately. But the circle didn't at first extend to other tribes. Indeed, wide acceptance of the idea that people of all nations have equal moral rights is quite recent.

How did it all happen? In one of Singer's later and less famous books, *The Expanding Circle* (Farrar, Straus, & Giroux, 1981), whose title refers to exactly this process, he writes as if the circle's expansion has been driven almost Platonically, by the "inherently expansionist nature of reasoning." Once people became civilized and started thinking about the logic behind the reciprocal extension of rights to one another, he says, they were on an intellectual "escalator," and there was no turning back. The idea of uniformly applied ethical strictures "emerges because of the social nature of human beings and the requirements of group living, but in the thought of reasoning beings, it takes on a logic of its own which leads to its extension beyond the bounds of the group."

This, alas, is perhaps too rosy a view. The concept of human rights has grown more inclusive largely through raw politics. Had tribes not found it in their interest to band together—sometimes to massacre other tribes—they wouldn't have had to invent the concept of inter-tribal rights. Necessity was similarly the mother of moral invention in modern societies. Had the suffragists not deftly wielded political clout, men mightn't have seen the logic of giving women the vote. Had the abolition of slavery not acquired political moment in a war that slaughtered millions, slavery might have long persisted.

Certainly in advances of this sort an important role can be played by intellectual persuasion, by sympathy, by empathy. These can fuse with political power and reinforce it. South Africa today exemplifies the mix. President F. W. de Klerk may or may not truly buy the moral logic behind his (relatively) progressive initiatives. But he definitely has felt the accompanying political pressure, ranging from international sanctions to domestic protest and unrest. On the other hand, behind those sanctions has been, among other things, some genuine empathy and some pure moral logic.

The bad news for animals is twofold. First, in all of these cases—women's rights, the abolition of slavery, ending apartheid—a good part of the political momentum comes from the oppressed themselves. Progress in South Africa never would have begun if blacks there hadn't perceived their own dignity and fought for it. Second, in all of these cases, empathy for the oppressed by influential outsiders came because the outsiders could identify with the oppressed—because, after all, they're people, too. With animal rights, in contrast, (1) the oppressed can never by themselves exert leverage; and (2) the outsiders who work on their behalf, belonging as they do to a different species, must be exquisitely, imaginatively compassionate in order to be drawn to the cause. To judge by history, this is not a recipe for success. It may forever remain the case that, when it comes time to sit down and do the moral bargaining, non-human animals, unlike all past downtrodden organisms, don't have much to bring to the table.

Notwithstanding these handicaps, the animal rights movement has made progress. American fur sales are by some accounts down (perhaps more out of fear of social disapproval than out of newfound sympathy). Some cosmetics companies have stopped abusing rabbits' eyes, finding that there are gentler ways to test products. And the university panels that administer federal laboratory regulations—designed to ensure that animal experimentation is worthwhile and not needlessly cruel—are undoubtedly, in the present climate, being at least as scrupulous as they've ever been (however scrupulous that is).

Even I—never quick to bring my deeds into sync with my words—am making minor gains. I hereby vow never again to eat veal. And it's conceivable that the dovetailing of moral concerns and health fears will get me to give up all red meat, among the most (formerly) sentient kind of flesh on the market. Also: no leather couches or leather jackets in my future. Shoes, yes, couches, no; the least we can do is distinguish between the functionally valuable and the frivolous. (Which also means, of course: people who wear fur coats to advertise their social status—which is to say all people who wear fur coats—should indeed, as the Humane Society's ads have it, be ashamed of themselves.) Finally, for what it's worth, I plan to keep intact my lifelong record of never eating pâté de foie gras, the preternaturally enlarged liver of a goose force-fed through a large tube.

But so long as I so much as eat tuna fish and support the use of primates in AIDS research, how can I still endorse the idea of human rights? How can I consider Stalin guilty of a moral crime and not just a utilitarian arithmetic error? One answer would be to admit that my allegiance to human rights isn't philosophical in the pure sense, but pragmatic; I've implicitly signed a non-aggression pact with all other humans, and Stalin violated the pact, which is immoral in this practical sense of the term. But I'd rather answer that, yes, I think moral law should be more than a deal cut among the powerful, but, no, I haven't been any more successful than the next guy in expunging all moral contradictions from my life. I'll try to do what I can.

If there is a half-decent excuse for this particular contradiction, I suppose it is that human civilization is moving in the right direction. Given where our moral thinking was 200, 500, 5,000 years ago, we're not doing badly. The expanding circle will never get as big as Singer would like, perhaps, but if it grows even slowly and fitfully, we'll be justified in taking a certain chauvinistic pride in our species.

Part Two

Animal Advocates and Their Critics

5

The Significance of Animal Suffering

Peter Singer

Nonhuman animals can suffer. To deny this, one must now refute not just the common sense of dog owners but the increasing body of empirical evidence, both physiological and behavioral (Dawkins 1980; Rollin 1989). My inquiry [here] takes the existence of animal suffering for granted. The question is: Does the suffering of nonhuman animals matter? If so, how much does it matter? When it comes to a choice between human welfare and the suffering of nonhuman animals, how should we choose?

Many people accept the following moral principles:

1. All humans are equal in moral status.
2. All humans are of superior moral status to nonhuman animals.

On the basis of these principles, it is commonly held that we should put human welfare ahead of the suffering of nonhuman animals; this assumption is reflected in our treatment of animals in many areas, including farming, hunting, experimentation, and entertainment. I shall argue the contrary: that the combination of the two principles cannot be defended within the terms of any convincing nonreligious approach to ethics. As a result, there is no rational ethical justification for always putting human suffering ahead of that of nonhuman animals.

From *Behavioral and Brain Sciences* 13, no. 1 (March 1980): 9–12. Copyright © 1980. Reprinted by permission of the author and Cambridge University Press.

Before I defend this claim, a word about religious ethics. It is of course no accident that the principle of human equality and the principle of animal inferiority are widely held in Western society. They reflect a Judeo-Christian view of the human-animal relationship. Genesis tells us that God gave human beings dominion over the beasts. This has generally been interpreted to mean that we human beings have divine warrant for always giving priority to human interests. A clear example can be seen in the work of William Paley, a progressive moral theologian of the late eighteenth century. He wrote that the practice of killing animals to eat them caused them pain and death for our pleasure and convenience; moreover, eating meat was unnecessary, since we could live on fruits and vegetables, as the Hindus do. We are therefore "beholden for it to the permission recorded in Scripture . . ." (Paley 1785). It is true that some Christians have argued for a very different interpretation of the Christian tradition, one much more favorable to nonhuman animals (Attfield 1983; Linzey 1987). But I am putting aside such theological questions, partly because there is no rational foundation for the premises on which they are based, and also because if we are considering public policy in a pluralistic society, we should not take a particular religious outlook as the basis for our laws.

Let us examine the two principles just stated. If they are to be held in combination, we can expect that there is some characteristic possessed by all human beings, but not possessed by any nonhuman animals, by virtue of which all human beings are equal, and nonhuman animals are less than equal to humans. But what might that characteristic be?

One possible answer to this question is that the characteristic is simply that of being human. But this merely invites a further question: Why does "being human" matter morally? Here we can go in either of two directions, depending on how we understand the term "human." On the one hand, the term can be used in a strict biological sense, so that it refers to members of the species *Homo sapiens;* on the other, it may refer to a being with those qualities which are distinctive of our species—in particular, the superior mental capacities that are characteristic of our species. Problems arise with both lines of response.

If the claim is that mere membership in the species *Homo sapiens* is enough to entitle a being to special moral consideration, we can reasonably ask why this should be so. Imagine that, as happens so often in science fiction, a good friend suddenly reveals that she is an alien who was stranded on earth when her spaceship crashed. Although she has been deceiving us all these years about her origins and her species, there was no deception in her visible delight in fresh spring mornings, her sorrow when she felt unloved, her concern for her friends, her dread of the dentist —all these feelings are real. Does our discovery about her species really make any difference as to how she should be treated? To say that it does is to make the mistake made by racists who think that blacks should be treated as inferiors, even though they acknowledge that blacks have the same interest as whites in being treated well. It is significant that there really are few such racists nowadays, and there were very few even when racism was defendeJ more often in public. That is because this type of racism depends so obviously on an arbitrary distinction. Yet a similar type of "speciesism" is still often encountered, either in its naked form, or thinly disguised under the claim that all human beings and only human beings possess some "intrinsic worth" or "dignity" not to be found in members of any other species (Bedau 1967; Frankena 1962). Generally no reasons are given for this claim, which resembles a religious incantation more than an argument. It is, in fact, a slightly secularized descendant of the Judeo-Christian belief that humans, and only humans, are made in the image of God; or the Christian view that only humans have immortal souls.

The term "speciesism" refers to the view that species membership is, *in itself,* a reason for giving more weight to the interests of one being than to those of another. This position, properly understood, is virtually never defended. Some who have claimed to be defending speciesism have in fact been defending a very different position: that there are morally relevant differences between species—such as differences in mental capacities—and that they entitle us to give more weight to the interests of members of the species with superior mental capacities (Cohen 1986). If this argument were successful, it would not justify speciesism, because the claim would not be that species membership *in itself* is a reason for giving more weight to the interests of one being than to those of another. The justification would be the difference in mental capacities, which happens to coincide with the difference in species. (The example of our friend the alien shows the difference; to a genuine speciesist, her mental capacities would be irrelevant; to a defender of the view we are now considering, they would be crucial.) The claim that there are morally relevant differences between all humans and other animals is the second way of understanding what it is to be "human": not the biological sense of membership in a species, but the sense in which to be human is to possess certain characteristics distinctive of our species, such as the capacities for self-awareness, for rationality, and for developing a moral sense.

It is easy to see why such characteristics should be morally relevant to how we treat a being. It is not arbitrary to say that beings with these capacities live fuller lives than beings without them, and that these beings therefore deserve a higher degree of consideration. (Note that I am not saying that this view is necessarily correct, but merely that—unlike the preference for members of a particular species merely on the grounds that they belong to that species—it is not arbitrary.)

There is, however, an obvious problem with any attempt to defend the principle of human equality by reference to superior mental capacities: they are not possessed by *all* humans. Newborn humans, for example, are not rational, appear not to be self-aware, cannot use language, do not share in culture or civilization, and have no sense of morality or justice. No doubt they have the potential to develop these characteristics, but arguing from potential is fraught with difficulties (Singer & Kuhse 1986; Singer & Dawson 1988). Moreover, if infants are to be brought within the scope of the principle of human equality by virtue of their potential, it would seem that human embryos and fetuses must also be included. This would require a significant revision of our attitudes to abortion and embryo research, although that in itself is not a reason for rejecting the appeal to potential. The real difficulty with the attempt to defend the principle of human equality on the grounds of superior mental capacities lies in the fact that even if we include those human beings with the potential to develop the requisite mental capacities, some humans will still be outside the scope of the principle of equality—those with profound and irreversible intellectual disabilities.

How are permanently, profoundly, intellectually disabled human beings to be included under the protection of the principle of human equality? One way would be to reduce the level of mental capacity required for inclusion. For example, if we were to require simply a capacity to feel pleasure or pain, to suffer or to enjoy life, almost all of the intellectually disabled could be included; those few who were excluded because they lack even this minimal capacity would be incapable of suffering by their exclusion. But whereas this would be acceptable as far as the principle of human equality is concerned, it would come into direct conflict with the principle of animal inferiority, because so many nonhuman animals would also satisfy the new standard.

No fine tuning of a standard based on mental capacities will eliminate the conflict between the two principles. Because there is an overlap between the capacities of human and nonhuman animals, there is no way would prefer—those lives as they will be lived if I do it, or those lives they will be lived if I do not. Thus, I must imagine myself as a pro- undly retarded child, as well as an evicted black parent, and as all the hers who will, to a greater or lesser degree, be affected by my decision. ace is not totally irrelevant here. When I imagine myself in the position the evicted blacks, I must consider what this experience would be like r a black person, whose attitudes have been shaped by a history of very and oppression. But having done my best to understand what the perience would be like for them, I do not then give their interests a ferent weight because they are the interests of black people. Similarly putting myself in the place of the profoundly retarded children, I can t ignore the fact that their mental capacities are different from those normal children, because this will affect the difference that my scheme l make to their lives. But after considering what experiencing this dif nce would be like, I do not then discount it because it is a difference de to the life of an intellectually disabled, rather than an intellectually e, person.

We should include animals in our moral reasoning in just the sam . To defend a proposal for improving the housing of battery hens he cost of making it more difficult for some families to afford eggs ould have to put myself into the positions of both the hens and th ilies. In trying to imagine what is it like to be a hen in a batter , compared with being a free-ranging hen, I would have to do m to grasp what it is like to be a hen, take into account everythin know about how a hen experiences confinement in a battery cag having done so (to the best of my ability), I would not then discou interests of the hen, on the grounds that hens are not human. Th acceptable limit to our moral concern is the point at which the awareness of pain or pleasure, no conscious preference, and hen apacity to experience suffering or happiness. That is why we nee nsider the interests of hens, but not those of lettuces. Hens can su ut lettuces cannot. (To the question as to where precisely the lim be drawn, I can only plead agnosticism. I presume that fish ca ain, but I do not know whether shrimps and insects can.)

To resolve such difficult questions as where to draw the boundari e capacity to suffer, or what individual animals of different speci rience,] we need all the assistance we can get. That is why the pi g work done by scientists such as Marian Stamp Dawkins (198 is so important. There are many methods of trying to assess wh

of drawing a line that will leave *all* human beings above the line, and *all* nonhumans below it.

At this point some observers make a different claim: that the issue should not be put in terms of whether all human beings individually pos- sess mental capacities that dogs lack, but rather whether the essential na- ture of humanity is different from the essential nature of, say, dogs. Thus rationality, or the capacity for making a moral judgment, or whatever else the capacity might be, is said to be an "essential feature" of humanity, but not of dogs; so even the most profoundly retarded human being is entitled to the respect and moral consideration that we properly deny to the most intelligent dog (Benn 1967; Cohen 1986).

What should we say about this shift of focus from the individual to the species? It is quite unclear what is meant by "essential feature" in this context; the term is redolent of an Aristotelian biology. We should not lose sight of the fact that whatever may be true of the "normal" adult human, there is nothing at all "rational" about the mental processes of some humans with congenital brain defects. It is therefore puzzling why we are supposed to treat them in ways appropriate to rational beings such as "normal" humans, rather than in ways appropriate to nonrational be- ings, such as some nonhuman animals.

Even if we were given a satisfactory explanation to end our puzzle- ment here, there is a good deal that should make us suspicious of the suggestion that we ignore individual characteristics and instead judge individuals by the general characteristics of their species. Just over a cen- tury ago a similar assertion was made by those who were against propo- sals to admit women to occupations such as law and medicine, and to the higher education that would qualify them for such professions. It was claimed that women, by their essential nature, lack the capacity for suc- cess in these areas. Against this claim, advocates of the feminist cause, John Stuart Mill among them, argued strongly that if the opponents of equality were successfully to make their case, they would have to main- tain that "the most eminent women are inferior in mental faculties to the most mediocre of the men on whom those functions at present devolve" (Mill 1970, p. 182). Surely Mill's claim is right; but note that it presup- poses that the focus is on the individual rather than on the group. If Mill's opponents were entitled to argue in terms of what is "normal" for men and women, or what is an "essential feature" of the sexes, Mill would have needed a different argument. He would have had to maintain that there are no differences in the essential nature of the sexes that affect the abilities required to succeed in the professions from which women were being excluded. Given the basic presuppositions of Mill's time (and perhaps even of our own), this would have been a much more difficult argument to sustain, and one that goes well beyond what is required for a successful attack on sexual discrimination in employment and education.

An important thrust of movements against discrimination has been the insistence that we consider individuals as such, and not as members of a group. It is curious that some writers want to reverse this in respect of humans and nonhuman animals, especially as they offer no clear reason why, in this particular case, we should focus on the species or kind, rather than on the individual. Indeed, the claim is simply asserted; no argument is presented in its defense. In the absence of any convincing reason for this claim, it should be rejected.

We are now in a position to see why it is so difficult to defend both the principle of human equality and that of animal inferiority. The key to the difficulty is that the combination of principles draws a sharp moral line, whereas evolution and natural variation have left an overlap between human beings and other animals. The solution is to abandon the attempt to draw such a sharp line. Instead, we should be sensitive to both the differences and the similarities between beings. Differences in such qualities as intelligence, self-awareness, and the capacity to make a moral judgment will certainly be relevant in some contexts; in others, similarities will be more important.

Up to this point my argument has had the limited aim of showing that we cannot justify applying sharply different standards to humans and nonhuman animals; but I have, strictly speaking, said nothing about my main subject, the significance of animal suffering. The statement that we should not apply different standards to humans and animals tells us nothing about what standard we should apply to both human and nonhuman animals. Someone might say, as scientists frequently do, that pain and suffering are part of nature, that they have evolved because they have survival value, and that there is no reason why we should be especially concerned with their reduction or elimination. I shall argue that, on the contrary, we should give to the elimination of the suffering of others—humans and nonhumans—the same degree of effort that we give to the elimination of similar suffering when it is our own. This is a demanding standard indeed, and it is only fair to say that although I regard the argument . . . up to this point as one which has proceeded quite rigorously, what follows is more controversial. It is a view that I hold in common

with a number of other philosophers, but also one with wh losophers disagree. Nevertheless, here are my reasons for hol

If we make a moral judgment, we must go beyond ou and preferences and base it on something more universal: we are prepared to accept as justifiable even if it should we lose by doing so. This conception of ethics is at the the most ancient ethical traditions, but it has been give expression in the work of contemporary philosophers (H Singer 1979; 1981). Although I may consider my own i first make an ethical judgment, I cannot give them greate because they are my own) than I give the interests of tl my judgment. If I do not condone robbery when I wo of it, then I cannot justify robbing someone if my victi a result of the robbery—unless there is some morally re between us that can be expressed in universal terms (that ifying the identity of the individual involved).

This method of ethical reasoning takes as its starti interests. The avoidance of suffering, therefore, receives ority in ethics as it does in all our lives, when it is o Other things being equal, it cannot be in my interests suffering, I must be in a state that, insofar as its *intri* concerned, I would rather not be in. (I specify intrinsic account of the objection that I may choose to suffe something else that I value; but if I could get that g ing, I would do so—or else it would not really be *s* choosing.) Conversely, to be happy is to be in a stat being equal, one would choose in preference to other of course, be other things that we value, or disvalue and suffering. The point is that once we understand th reasoning, the significance of suffering and happiness i

It is consistent both with the method of ethical re and with the argument presented in the first part of weight we give to the interests of others should not sex, or species. Suppose that I have suddenly conceiv od of dramatically improving the lives of profoun languishing in state institutions, but to implement poverty-stricken black families from a building I ow I ought to do this, I must imagine myself as living affected to any degree by my decision, and ask w

an experience is like for a being who cannot describe it to us. Before any empirical attempts at such assessment were made, we could rely on the knowledge of those who knew the animals well and had observed them over long periods. They were often able to understand empathetically what the animals were feeling. But such reports were subjective, based on signs that the observer was perhaps unable to describe. When methods of farm production worth billions of dollars annually were challenged by people concerned about animal welfare, these reports from people with lifetimes of experience were often rejected as "subjective" and "unscientific." But what else could humans do to put themselves in the animals' positions? They could measure productivity, observe instances of abnormal behavior, examine the animals' physical health, or test the levels of hormones in their blood; yet these were all very indirect ways of understanding what the animals themselves felt about different situations. Dawkins's approach has its own methodological problems, as she acknowledges; but it gives us new and valuable information that, perhaps more directly than any other "objective" method, enables us to form some idea of what an experience is really like for the animal at the center of it. And this, as we have just seen, is at the core of ethical reasoning about our treatment of animals. It is because suffering, whether human or nonhuman, is ethically significant that we must welcome new insights into the existence, and degree, of that suffering.

REFERENCES

Attfield, R. (1983) *The Ethics of Environmental Concern.* Blackwell.

Bedau, H. A. (1967) "Egalitarianism and the Idea of Equality." In: *Nomos IX: Equality,* ed. J. R. Pennock and J. W. Chapman. Atherton Press.

Benn, S. (1967) "Egalitarianism and Equal Consideration of Interests. In: *Nomos IX: Equality,* ed. J. R. Pennock and J. W. Chapman. Atherton Press.

Cohen, C. (1986) "The Case for the Use of Animals in Biomedical Research." *New England Journal of Medicine* 315:865–70. [See selection 10 in this volume.]

Dawkins, M. S. (1980) *Animal Suffering: The Science of Animal Welfare.* Chapman & Hall.

———(1989) "Time Budgets in Red Junglefowl as a Baseline for the Assessment of Welfare in Domestic Fowl," *Applied Animal Behaviour Science* 24:77–80.

Frankena, W. (1962) "The Concept of Social Justice." In: *Social Justice,* ed. R. Brandt. Prentice-Hall.

Hare, R. M.. (1963) *Freedom and Reason.* Oxford University Press.
———. (1981) *Moral Thinking: Its Levels, Method, and Point.* Clarendon Press.
Linzey, A. (1987) *Christianity and the Rights of Animals.* Society for the Propagation of Christian Knowledge, London.
Mill, J. S. (1970) *The Subjection of Women.* [First published 1869.] Reprinted in: *Essays on Sex Equality,* ed. A. Rossi. University of Chicago Press.
Paley, W. (1785) *Principles of Moral and Political Philosophy.* Baldwin & Company.
Rollin, B. E. (1989) *The Unheeded Cry.* Oxford University Press.
Singer, P. (1979) *Practical Ethics.* Cambridge University Press.
———. (1981) *The Expanding Circle.* Farrar, Straus & Giroux.
Singer, P. and Dawson, K. (1988) "IVF Technology and the Argument from Potential." *Philosophy and Public Affairs* 17:87–104.
Singer, P. and Kuhse, H. (1986) "The Ethics of Embryo Research." *Law, Medicine, and Health Care* 14:133–38.

6

In Defense of Speciesism

J. A. Gray

Singer's ethical proposals . . . aim at universality, and thus follow a prestigious philosophical tradition. . . . He states that, though it is right to take into account special features of the particular species to which an individual belongs (and also special features characteristic of the particular individual concerned) in assessing the degree of suffering it experiences under given circumstances, it is morally wrong to give any weight to such features in choosing between the suffering that might be experienced by different individuals. Singer states that "in trying to imagine what it is like being a hen in a battery cage, as compared with being a free-ranging hen, I would have to do my best to grasp what it is like to be a hen, taking into account everything we know about how a hen experiences confinement in a battery cage; but having done this (to the best of my ability) I would not then discount the interests of the hen, on the grounds that they are not human." To discount an animal's interests on the grounds that the animal is not human is to be guilty of "speciesism"—"the view that species is, *in itself,* a reason for giving more weight to the interests of one being than another." According to Singer, "this position, properly understood, is virtually never defended." If this is so, it is unfortunate, since (philosophers and extremist members of animal rights movements

From *Behavioral and Brain Sciences* 13, no. 1 (March 1980): 22–23. Copyright © 1980. Reprinted by permission of the author and Cambridge University Press.

apart) I would guess that the view that human beings matter to other human beings more than animals do is, to say the least, widespread. At any rate, I wish to defend speciesism here.

Let me begin by distinguishing between ethical principles and moral choices. I do not wish to question the view that ethical principles should not be qualified by species. If it is wrong to inflict pain unnecessarily, it is equally wrong whether the pain is inflicted upon a human being, a rat, or a spider. But the situation is quite different when it comes to moral choices between suffering experienced by human beings and that experienced by members of other species; indeed, the situation is already quite different when it comes to choosing between the suffering of two different individuals even if both belong to the human species.

Consider an extreme version of the latter case, in which the degree of suffering can be considered identical for the two individuals concerned. A mother is faced with the choice of saving one of two small children from a fire, knowing that the other will die. Suppose that one of the children is her own and that, as is most likely, this is the one she saves. Few would find this choice morally reprehensible; the alternative choice would likely be seen as a failure in the mother's primary duty to her own child. Suppose that we now relax the condition of identical suffering for the two children: The mother has to choose between a burn of lesser severity inflicted upon her own child and one of greater severity inflicted on the other. Or suppose that the two children in some sense have different qualities of life: The mother's own child is crippled, mentally handicapped, or shows dangerous psychotic tendencies, whereas the other is healthy and normal. No doubt, a point would come at which the imbalance between the two children or their degrees of suffering would outweigh the initial bias in favor of the mother's own child; but few would find it morally unacceptable if the required degree of imbalance turned out to be rather large, as I imagine it would in most real cases.

We may be reasonably certain that the origin of both the mother's most likely choice and our most likely reaction to this choice, is biological; the forces of natural selection have shaped the ways in which we interact with one another to maximize survival of the genes we carry. One reaction to such an understanding of the biological origin of the mother's choice might be to remove it entirely from the sphere of moral action. We do not, after all, regard the murder of a sexual rival as morally acceptable on the grounds that it stems from the same biological orgin. But this reaction would, I believe, be a mistake. Most of the behavior that is normally regarded as morally desirable was part of our biological heritage before it was codified and transformed by moral philosophers. If the discovery of a biological origin for such behavior is suficient to remove it from the moral sphere, there may in the end be little left of morality. Much of the concern we feel for the welfare of people unrelated to ourselves is very likely to be an extension of the genetically based concerns that we feel for kin; a further extension of the same type of concern may well contribute to the animal welfare movement. (Consider how much easier it is to arouse sympathy for mammals that resemble us than for fish, which do not.)

The mother's choice in the example just given is not as different as it may at first seem from the choices that have to be made with regard to the proper human use of animals. If we are guided simply by an ethical principle of universal applicability—for example, that it is wrong to inflict pain, without regard to species—then experiments that would not be permitted with human subjects ought not to be carried out with animals. But there are also moral choices that have to be made. In many cases the decision not to carry out certain experiments with animals (even if they would inflict pain or suffering) is likely to have the consequence that some people will undergo pain or suffering that might otherwise be avoided. Suppose that we could measure the degrees of suffering inflicted upon the animals and people concerned, and that we came to the conclusion that these were exactly equal. The "speciesist" claim is that under such circumstances the calculus of suffering should give more weight to one side of the equation *just because* it pertains to human beings. This claim, I believe, can be coherently defended on the grounds that, just as a mother owes a special duty to her child (and for the same kind of biologically based reasons), so we owe a special duty to members of our own species. It would therefore, in the example given, be morally right to carry out the experiments concerned.

As in the case of the mother, we may now relax the condition of equality for suffering for animals and for human beings. Equality of suffering would result if the severity of the experiments to human beings were reduced. A complication is that the benefit to human beings may not be the direct alleviation of suffering (thus compounding still further the problems of comparison that arise even if the equation for both species is couched in terms of suffering alone). Even if the aim of an experiment is, in the long run, the alleviation of human suffering, it is usually only after the extensive development of knowledge and scientific understanding in a particular field that medical advance becomes possible; in the interim, the advancement of scientific understanding may be the only specific objective that the experiment can readily attain. (A case can also be made that an understanding of the biological world to which we belong is itself an aim of sufficient moral worth to justify the imposition of suffering; but that case is peripheral to the arguments pursued here.) However complex the calculus, there will at some point be a degree of imbalance at which the suffering inflicted upon animals is too great to be worth the avoidance of lesser suffering (or provision of other benefit) by people. Exactly how great that imbalance has to be (after every possible step has been taken to minimize unnecessary suffering) is at the core of the often very difficult decisions that have to be made by scientists and by the ethical committees that (thanks in large measure to the proper concerns of people like Singer) now increasingly watch over their activities. . . .

7

The Attribution of Suffering

William Timberlake

A fundamental problem with Singer's [essay] is the lack of an adequate definition of suffering. Though a central aim of the animal welfare movement is to reduce or eliminate suffering in animals, [Singer has] given us only the most tentative grounds for discovering and analyzing it. Animal suffering has become so emotionally charged a term that attempts to analyze it critically have been rejected in favor of immediate action to stop it. But if animal welfare advocates aspire to be more than a lay-oriented animal rights group whose members are scientists, they must determine when and how much animals suffer.

THE DEFINITION AND DETERMINANTS OF SUFFERING

A major contention of animal rights groups is that suffering in animals is easily inferred from simple criteria and that all animal research involves animal suffering. Most scientists have difficulty taking these claims seriously. There is no definition or analysis of suffering, and rarely do such groups present the convergent evidence required for attributing suffering in humans. Most of us have learned from experience not to infer too

From *Behavioral and Brain Sciences* 13, no. 1 (March 1980): 36–39. Copyright © 1980. Reprinted by permission of the author and Cambridge University Press.

readily that people who have artificial body parts, or live more than two to a room, or eat fewer than three meals a day are suffering. But if an animal has on a head cap, is restricted in its access to food, or is in a cage, it is presumed to suffer. The animal rights approach also completely ignores the scientific context of experimentation, including potential uses of the results; the scientist's aversion to causing needless pain and wasting time and resources on experiments with animals that are not healthy and well cared for; and the limitations on experimentation imposed by the institutional review of experiments according to the Public Health Service guidelines. But scientists have underestimated the impact of the sheer repetition of activists' claims on a willing press. Because there is no agreement on a formal definition of suffering, there has been little coherent disputation of the claim that all animal experimentation produces suffering and must therefore be immediately stopped.

Unfortunately, attempts by lawmakers and animal welfare advocates to define suffering have usually been unidimensional and biased on the side of sensitivity. For example, rules recently proposed by the United States Department of Agriculture governing the transportation of all nonhuman primates require, among other things, that animals never be exposed to temperatures over 85°F, that they be exposed to temperatures over 75°F for a maximum of four hours a day and only if efforts are made to lower the temperature, and that they never be in visual contact with any nonhuman mammal. The United Kingdom's Farm Animal Welfare Council has endorsed the view that animals suffer when they are unable to perform the full repertoire of behavior shown by members of their species "in nature."

Though these rules and assumptions arise from the best of motives, consider that: (1) at least half of the humans on this planet are regularly exposed to these circumstances without reported large-scale suffering; (2) the great majority of pets have been exposed to these circumstances, yet most of their owners do not consider that their pets have suffered; (3) these circumstances regularly exist for many natural populations, again without any supposition that we should do something about them. What is even more remarkable is that in most cases there is almost no evidence indicating that the prescribed rules are effective in reducing suffering, or even which circumstances are preferred by the animals involved.

These rules and assumptions come closest to what highly protective parents might desire for their children, but would not see enacted into law because of the cost and lack of agreement as to what was best for children. Somehow, self-appointed parents of research animals have convinced lawmakers that they know best, and as the head of policy-making at the USDA remarked, cost is not a concern. As a result, many standards of animal care are higher than those for workplaces, day-care centers, schools, nursing homes, and, in some respects, even hospitals. It could be argued that in the best of all possible worlds we should all be treated with equal extreme care. In a complex world in which children die of hunger and many people are poisoned by pollutants, however, it seems that, at the least, we have gotten our priorities in the wrong order.

SINGER'S CLAIMS

Singer, like other animal rights advocates, is not concerned with the definition of suffering. Rather, his concern is that animal suffering exists and that we should treat it the same as our own suffering. At first glance, failing to distinguish between the suffering of humans and the suffering of ticks, tapeworms, and maggots does not seem like a plausible position. There are hints that Singer intends ultimately to measure the intensity of suffering to make difficult decisions about relative suffering. But this is not included in the form of his main arguments, and it is certainly not the way his arguments have been used by animal rights advocates.

Singer begins with the assumption that animal suffering is rampant because of our Judeo-Christian heritage, which gives humans "dominion" over animals. According to Singer, in this tradition "humans beings have a divine warrant for always giving priority to human interests." I am neither a biblical scholar nor a historian, but as I remember it, the meaning of dominion here implies responsibility as well as authority. Certainly farmers who espouse the Judeo-Christian ethic have risked their lives for their animals, and provided them at times with equal or even privileged access to scarce resources of food and shelter. I believe that the concern of many ecologists about disappearing species comes partly from a sense of the responsibility of human dominion over the planet. The animal rights movement itself appears to have roots in the Judeo-Christian beliefs of the unique responsibility of humans for animals and the obligation to deny impulses to gain advantage over those who are less powerful than ourselves.

Singer attacks the Judeo-Christian ethic for producing two highly influential but contradictory moral principles: (1) All humans are equal in moral status; (2) all humans are superior in moral status to nonhuman animals. According to Singer, these assumptions are incompatible because their joint truth requires the existence of some common quality that is possessed by humans, making them equal, and is not possessed by animals. Singer then argues that because there is no such quality, we must give the same effort to the elimination of suffering in animals as we do to the elimination of suffering in humans.

There are many problems with this approach. First, I'm not clear these are common assumptions. I do not believe that people commonly assume that all humans are equal in moral status or even that all humans are better than all animals. Equality of moral status is something we aspire to in specific circumstances; we have tried to formalize those circumstances in legal systems, but a few moments of conversation with the average person should convince one that this is not a common belief. Children do not have the moral status of adults, the mentally ill are not judged by the same standards as the mentally competent, illegal immigrants do not have the moral status of citizens, nonresident poor do not have the moral status of resident poor, strangers do not have the moral status of friends, someone who has stolen from us does not have the moral status of someone who has befriended us. A fairer summary of what we commonly believe is that only within certain boundaries and in certain dimensions are humans assumed to be similar in moral status, and usually only in the absence of further information.

I believe we commonly place nonhuman animals in the same framework. For example, both people and animals that are judged nobler or more intelligent are often accorded higher moral status. In a not inconsequential number of cases, some animals may be viewed as nobler than some or even most humans. When we add to this an overall bias toward viewing beings that are more similar to or related to ourselves as nobler or more intelligent than beings that are distantly removed from us, we have a complex set of assumptions influencing the judgments of differences in the moral status of both human and nonhuman animals. There is no necessary discontinuity between our moral evaluations of animals and humans and, thus, no logical problem. Both human and nonhuman animals may be ranked differently and with overlap in moral status depending on the dimensions and circumstances.

The second problem with Singer's approach is that there *is* a common quality that unites humans and separates them from animals, namely, the unique aspects of DNA found in human cells. Singer might well argue here that we cannot specify perfectly the nature of the human gene pool, and that even if we could, it would simply be a species identification and not a logical reason for making judgments of the relative value of suffering. As far as I can see, however, the existence of even modestly distinct pools of DNA must be based on pressures toward reproduction within that restricted set of genes. At least some of this pressure will take the form of choices that effectively value the suffering and survival of gene pool representatives more than the suffering, survival, and reproduction of some other set of animals having an alternative gene pool. If this is not so, either the amount of resources in the world is infinite, or the particular gene pool in question will not long be with us.

I am not arguing that all acts necessarily have immediate or even long-term benefits to a particular gene pool. Social species, perhaps especially humans, make choices that benefit the survival and reproduction of genetically dissimilar animals. But the variables controlling these acts of altruism more often than not do produce results of long-term benefit to the human gene pool. Thus, though all acts of individual animals may not contribute to the reproduction of their own genes, if we consider all acts controlled by similar variables across all individuals from a gene pool, that is the expected direction.

Singer might well acknowledge that this is the status of the world, yet argue that it should be different. The moral status and suffering of an animal should count the same as those of humans to every human evaluator. Appealing though it may be, this view is neither logically consistent nor viable. Consider the incompatibility of the following beliefs: (1) All animals (including humans) are equal in moral status; (2) all animals except humans can promote the survival of their own kind at the expense of the suffering and restricted access to resources of other species. First, it follows from statement (1) that humans have the same rights as predators to express their predatory tendencies. But it follows from statement (2) that they must not express these tendencies. Therefore, the moral status of humans is either higher or lower than that of other animals, but definitely different.

A second argument is similar. On the grounds of evolution, the rule that all animals are equal in moral status is literally not viable. Every animal on the planet is competing for resources with other animals. Even the most devout human vegetarian living alone with minimal shelter, few clothes, and great respect for life is denying resources critical to the survival and reproduction of a surprisingly large number of animals by his simple presence in the ecosystem. If he has a dog or a cat as a pet, so much the worse for other animals.

In short, the logic of our Judeo-Christian heritage is certainly no more flawed than that of the animal rights approach (which in part represents an extension of pieces of that heritage). Both animal rights advocates and scientists want to reduce the suffering of others, but this cannot be done in any reasonable way until we agree on its nature, extent, and relative value.

8

The Case for Animal Rights

Tom Regan

I regard myself as an advocate of animal rights—as a part of the animal rights movement. That movement, as I conceive it, is committed to a number of goals, including:

- the total abolition of the use of animals in science;
- the total dissolution of commercial animal agriculture;
- the total elimination of commercial and sport hunting and trapping.

There are, I know, people who profess to believe in animal rights but do not avow these goals. Factory farming, they say, is wrong—it violates animals' rights—but traditional animal agriculture is all right. Toxicity tests of cosmetics on animals violates their rights, but important medical research—cancer research, for example—does not. The clubbing of baby seals is abhorrent, but not the harvesting of adult seals. I used to think I understood this reasoning. Not any more. You don't change unjust institutions by tidying them up.

What's wrong—fundamentally wrong—with the way animals are treated isn't the details that vary from case to case. It's the whole system. The forlornness of the veal calf is pathetic, heart wrenching; the pulsing

From *In Defence of Animals*, edited by Peter Singer (Oxford: Basil Blackwell, 1985), pp. 13–26. Reprinted by permission of the author and the publisher.

pain of the chimp with electrodes planted deep in her brain is repulsive; the slow, torturous death of the raccoon caught in the leg-hold trap is agonizing. But what is wrong isn't the pain, isn't the suffering, isn't the deprivation. These compound what's wrong. Sometimes—often—they make it much, much worse. But they are not the fundamental wrong.

The fundamental wrong is the system that allows us to view animals as *our resources,* here for *us*—to be eaten, or surgically manipulated, or exploited for sport or money. Once we accept this view of animals—as our resources—the rest is as predictable as it is regrettable. Why worry about their loneliness, their pain, their death? Since animals exist for us, to benefit us in one way or another, what harms them really doesn't matter —or matters only if it starts to bother us, makes us feel a trifle uneasy. . . .

In the case of animals in science, whether and how we abolish their use . . . are to a large extent political questions. People must change their beliefs before they change their habits. Enough people, especially those elected to public office, must believe in change—must want it—before we will have laws that protect the rights of animals. This process of change is very complicated, very demanding, very exhausting, calling for the efforts of many hands in education, publicity, political organization and activity, down to the licking of envelopes and stamps. As a trained and practicing philosopher, the sort of contribution I can make is limited but, I like to think, important. The currency of philosophy is ideas—their meaning and rational foundation—not the nuts and bolts of the legislative process, say, or the mechanics of community organization. That's what I have been exploring over the past ten years or so in my essays and talks and, most recently, in my book, *The Case for Animal Rights.* I believe the major conclusions I reach in the book are true because they are supported by the weight of the best arguments. I believe the idea of animal rights has reason, not just emotion, on its side.

In the space I have at my disposal here I can only sketch, in the barest outline, some of the main features of the book. Its main themes— and we should not be surprised by this—involve asking and answering deep, foundational moral questions about what morality is, how it should be understood and what is the best moral theory, all considered. I hope I can convey something of the shape I think this theory takes. The attempt to do this will be (to use a word a friendly critic once used to describe my work) cerebral, perhaps too cerebral. But this is misleading. My feelings about how animals are sometimes treated run just as deep and just as strong as those of my more volatile compatriots. Philosophers do—

to use the jargon of the day have a right side to their brains. If it's the left side we contribute (or mainly should), that's because what talents we have reside there.

How to proceed? We begin by asking how the moral status of animals has been understood by thinkers who deny that animals have rights. Then we test the mettle of their ideas by seeing how well they stand up under the heat of fair criticism. If we start our thinking in this way, we soon find that some people believe that we have no duties directly to animals, that we owe nothing to them, that we can do nothing that wrongs them. Rather, we can do wrong acts that involve animals, and so we have duties regarding them, though none to them. Such views may be called indirect duty views. By way of illustration: suppose your neighbor kicks your dog. Then your neighbor has done something wrong. But not to your dog. The wrong that has been done is a wrong to you. After all, it is wrong to upset people, and your neighbor's kicking your dog upsets you. So you are the one who is wronged, not your dog. Or again: by kicking your dog your neighbor damages your property. And since it is wrong to damage another person's property, your neighbor has done something wrong—to you, of course, not to your dog. Your neighbor no more wrongs your dog than your car would be wronged if the windshield were smashed. Your neighbor's duties involving your dog are indirect duties to you. More generally, all of our duties regarding animals are indirect duties to one another—to humanity.

How could someone try to justify such a view? Someone might say that your dog doesn't feel anything and so isn't hurt by your neighbor's kick, doesn't care about the pain since none is felt, is as unaware of anything as is your windshield. Someone might say this, but no rational person will, since, among other considerations, such a view will commit anyone who holds it to the position that no human being feels pain either—that human beings also don't care about what happens to them. A second possibility is that though both humans and your dog are hurt when kicked, it is only human pain that matters. But, again, no rational person can believe this. Pain is pain wherever it occurs. If your neighbor's causing you pain is wrong because of the pain that is caused, we cannot rationally ignore or dismiss the moral relevance of the pain that your dog feels.

Philosophers who hold indirect duty views—and many still do—have come to understand that they must avoid the two defects just noted: that is, both the view that animals don't feel anything as well as the idea that only human pain can be morally relevant. Among such thinkers

the sort of view now favored is one or other form of what is called
contractarianism.

Here, very crudely, is the root idea: morality consists of a set of rules
that individuals voluntarily agree to abide by, as we do when we sign
a contract (hence the name contractarianism). Those who understand and
accept the terms of the contract are covered directly; they have rights created and recognized by, and protected in, the contract. And these contractors can also have protection spelled out for others who, though they
lack the ability to understand morality and so cannot sign the contract
themselves, are loved or cherished by those who can. Thus young children,
for example, are unable to sign contracts and lack rights. But they are
protected by the contract nonetheless because of the sentimental interests
of others, most notably their parents. So we have, then, duties involving
these children, duties regarding them, but no duties to them. Our duties
in their case are indirect duties to other human beings, usually their parents.

As for animals, since they cannot understand contracts, they obviously cannot sign; and since they cannot sign, they have no rights. Like
children, however, some animals are the objects of the sentimental interest of others. You, for example, love your dog or cat. So those animals
that enough people care about (companion animals, whales, baby seals,
the American bald eagle), though they lack rights themselves, will be protected because of the sentimental interests of people. I have, then, according to contractarianism, no duty directly to your dog or any other animal,
not even the duty not to cause them pain or suffering; my duty not to
hurt them is a duty I have to those people who care about what happens
to them. As for other animals, where no or little sentimental interest is
present—in the case of farm animals, for example, or laboratory rats—
what duties we have grow weaker and weaker, perhaps to vanishing point.
The pain and death they endure, though real, are not wrong if no one
cares about them.

When it comes to the moral status of animals, contractarianism could
be a hard view to refute if it were an adequate theoretical approach to
the moral status of human beings. It is not adequate in this latter respect,
however, which makes the question of its adequacy in the former case,
regarding animals, utterly moot. For consider: morality, according to the
(crude) contractarian position before us, consists of rules that people agree
to abide by. What people? Well, enough to make a difference—enough,
that is, *collectively* to have the power to enforce the rules that are drawn
up in the contract. That is very well and good for the signatories but

not so good for anyone who is not asked to sign. And there is nothing in contractarianism of the sort we are discussing that guarantees or requires that everyone will have a chance to participate equally in framing the rules of morality. The result is that this approach to ethics could sanction the most blatant forms of social, economic, moral and political injustice, ranging from a repressive caste system to systematic racial or sexual discrimination. Might, according to this theory, does make right. Let those who are the victims of injustice suffer as they will. It matters not so long as no one else—no contractor, or too few of them—cares about it. Such a theory takes one's moral breath away . . . as if, for example, there would be nothing wrong with apartheid in South Africa if few white South Africans were upset by it. A theory with so little to recommend it at the level of the ethics of our treatment of our fellow humans cannot have anything more to recommend it when it comes to the ethics of how we treat our fellow animals.

The version of contractarianism just examined is, as I have noted, a crude variety, and in fairness to those of a contractarian persuasion it must be noted that much more refined, subtle and ingenious varieties are possible. For example, John Rawls, in his *A Theory of Justice,* sets forth a version of contractarianism that forces contractors to ignore the accidental features of being a human being—for example, whether one is white or black, male or female, a genius or of modest intellect. Only by ignoring such features, Rawls believes, can we ensure that the principles of justice that contractors would agree upon are not based on bias or prejudice. Despite the improvement a view such as Rawls's represents over the cruder forms of contractarianism, it remains deficient: it systematically denies that we have direct duties to those human beings who do not have a sense of justice—young children, for instance, and many mentally retarded humans. And yet it seems reasonably certain that, were we to torture a young child or a retarded elder, we would be doing something that wronged him or her, not something that would be wrong if (and only if) other humans with a sense of justice were upset. And since this is true in the case of these humans, we cannot rationally deny the same in the case of animals.

Indirect duty views, then, including the best among them, fail to command our rational assent. Whatever ethical theory we should accept rationally, therefore, it must at least recognize that we have some duties directly to animals, just as we have some duties directly to each other. . . .

Some people think that the theory we are looking for is utilitarianism. A utilitarian accepts two moral principles. The first is that of equality: everyone's interests count, and similar interests must be counted as having similar weight or importance. White or black, American or Iranian, human or animal—everyone's pain or frustration matter, and matter just as much as the equivalent pain or frustration of anyone else. The second principle a utilitarian accepts is that of utility: do the act that will bring about the best balance between satisfaction and frustration for everyone affected by the outcome.

As a utilitarian, then, here is how I am to approach the task of deciding what I morally ought to do: I must ask who will be affected if I choose to do one thing rather than another, how much each individual will be affected, and where the best results are most likely to lie—which option, in other words, is most likely to bring about the best results, the best balance between satisfaction and frustration. That option, whatever it may be, is the one I ought to choose. That is where my moral duty lies.

The great appeal of utilitarianism rests with its uncompromising *egalitarianism:* everyone's interests count and count as much as the like interests of everyone else. The kind of odious discrimination that some forms of contractarianism can justify—discrimination based on race or sex, for example—seems disallowed in principle by utilitarianism, as is speciesism, systematic discrimination based on species membership.

The equality we find in utilitarianism, however, is not the sort an advocate of animal or human rights should have in mind. Utilitarianism has no room for the equal moral rights of different individuals because it has no room for their equal inherent value or worth. What has value for the utilitarian is the satisfaction of an individual's interests, not the individual whose interests they are. A universe in which you satisfy your desire for water, food and warmth is, other things being equal, better than a universe in which these desires are frustrated. And the same is true in the case of an animal with similar desires. But neither you nor the animal have any value in your own right. Only your feelings do.

Here is an analogy to help make the philosophical point clearer: a cup contains different liquids, sometimes sweet, sometimes bitter, sometimes a mix of the two. What has value are the liquids: the sweeter the better, the bitterer the worse. The cup, the container, has no value. It is what goes into it, not what they go into, that has value. For the utilitarian you and I are like the cup; we have no value as individuals and thus no equal value. What has value is what goes into us, what we serve as receptacles for; our feelings of satisfaction have positive value, our feelings of frustration negative value.

Serious problems arise for utilitarianism when we remind ourselves that it enjoins us to bring about the best consequences. What does this mean? It doesn't mean the best consequences for me alone, or for my family or friends, or any other person taken individually. No, what we must do is, roughly, as follows: we must add up (somehow!) the separate satisfactions and frustrations of everyone likely to be affected by our choice, the satisfactions in one column, the frustrations in the other. We must total each column for each of the options before us. That is what it means to say the theory is aggregative. And then we must choose that option which is most likely to bring about the best balance of totaled satisfactions over totaled frustrations. Whatever act would lead to this outcome is the one we ought morally to perform—it is where our moral duty lies. And that act quite clearly might not be the same one that would bring about the best results for me personally, or for my family or friends, or for a lab animal. The best aggregated consequences for everyone concerned are not necessarily the best for each individual.

That utilitarianism is an aggregative theory—different individuals' satisfactions or frustrations are added, or summed, or totaled—is the key objection to this theory. My Aunt Bea is old, inactive, a cranky, sour person, though not physically ill. She prefers to go on living. She is also rather rich. I could make a fortune if I could get my hands on her money, money she intends to give me in any event, after she dies, but which she refuses to give me now. In order to avoid a huge tax bite, I plan to donate a handsome sum of my profits to a local children's hospital. Many, many children will benefit from my generosity, and much joy will be brought to their parents, relatives and friends. If I don't get the money rather soon, all these ambitions will come to naught. The once-in-a-life-time opportunity to make a real killing will be gone. Why, then, not kill my Aunt Bea? Oh, of course I *might* get caught. But I'm no fool and, besides, her doctor can be counted on to cooperate (he has an eye for the same investment and I happen to know a good deal about his shady past). The deed can be done . . . professionally, shall we say. There is *very* little chance of getting caught. And as for my conscience being guilt-ridden, I am a resourceful sort of fellow and will take more than sufficient comfort—as I lie on the beach at Acapulco—in contemplating the joy and health I have brought to so many others.

Suppose Aunt Bea is killed and the rest of the story comes out as told. Would I have done anything wrong? Anything immoral? One would have thought that I had. Not according to utilitarianism. Since what I have done has brought about the best balance between totaled satisfaction and frustration for all those affected by the outcome, my action is not wrong. Indeed, in killing Aunt Bea the physician and I did what duty required.

This same kind of argument can be repeated in all sorts of cases, illustrating, time after time, how the utilitarian's position leads to results that impartial people find morally callous. It *is* wrong to kill my Aunt Bea in the name of bringing about the best results for others. A good end does not justify an evil means. Any adequate moral theory will have to explain why this is so. Utilitarianism fails in this respect and so cannot be the theory we seek.

What to do? Where to begin anew? The place to begin, I think, is with the utilitarian's view of the value of the individual—or, rather, lack of value. In its place, suppose we consider that you and I, for example, do have value as individuals—what we'll call *inherent value*. To say we have such value is to say that we are something more than, something different from, mere receptacles. Moreover, to ensure that we do not pave the way for such injustices as slavery or sexual discrimination, we must believe that all who have inherent value have it equally, regardless of their sex, race, religion, birthplace and so on. Similarly to be discarded as irrelevant are one's talents or skills, intelligence and wealth, personality or pathology, whether one is loved and admired or despised and loathed. The genius and the retarded child, the prince and the pauper, the brain surgeon and the fruit vendor, Mother Teresa and the most unscrupulous used-car salesman—all have inherent value, all possess it equally, and all have an equal right to be treated with respect, to be treated in ways that do not reduce them to the status of things, as if they existed as resources for others. My value as an individual is independent of my usefulness to you. Yours is not dependent on your usefulness to me. For either of us to treat the other in ways that fail to show respect for the other's independent value is to act immorally, to violate the individual's rights.

Some of the rational virtues of this view—what I call the rights view —should be evident. Unlike (crude) contractarianism, for example, the rights view *in principle* denies the moral tolerability of any and all forms of racial, sexual or social discrimination; and unlike utilitarianism, this view *in principle* denies that we can justify good results by using evil means that violate an individual's rights—denies, for example, that it could be moral to kill my Aunt Bea to harvest beneficial consequences for others. That would be to sanction the disrespectful treatment of the individual in the name of the social good, something the rights view will not— categorically will not—ever allow.

The rights view, I believe, is rationally the most satisfactory moral theory. It surpasses all other theories in the degree to which it illuminates and explains the foundation of our duties to one another—the domain of human morality. On this score it has the best reasons, the best arguments, on its side. Of course, if it were possible to show that only human beings are included within its scope, then a person like myself, who believes in animal rights, would be obliged to look elsewhere.

But attempts to limit its scope to humans only can be shown to be rationally defective. Animals, it is true, lack many of the abilities humans possess. They can't read, do higher mathematics, build a bookcase or make *baba ghanoush*. Neither can many human beings, however, and yet we don't (and shouldn't) say that they (these humans) therefore have less inherent value, less of a right to be treated with respect, than do others. It is the *similarities* between those human beings who most clearly, most non-controversially have such value (the people reading this, for example), not our differences, that matter most. And the really crucial, the basic similarity is simply this: we are each of us the experiencing subject of a life, a conscious creature having an individual welfare that has importance to us whatever our usefulness to others. We want and prefer things, believe and feel things, recall and expect things. And all these dimensions of our life, including our pleasure and pain, our enjoyment and suffering, our satisfaction and frustration, our continued existence or our untimely death—all make a difference to the quality of our life as lived, as experienced, by us as individuals. As the same is true of those animals that concern us, . . . they too must be viewed as the experiencing subjects of a life, with inherent value of their own.

Some there are who resist the idea that animals have inherent value. "Only humans have such value," they profess. How might this narrow view be defended? Shall we say that only humans have the requisite intelligence, or autonomy, or reason? But there are many, many humans who fail to meet these standards and yet are reasonably viewed as having value above and beyond their usefulness to others. Shall we claim that only humans belong to the right species, the species *Homo sapiens?* But this is blatant speciesism. Will it be said, then, that all—and only—humans have immortal souls? Then our opponents have their work cut out for them. I am myself not ill-disposed to the proposition that there are immortal souls. Personally, I profoundly hope I have one. But I would not want to rest my position on a controversial ethical issue on the even more controversial question about who or what has an immortal soul. That is to dig one's hole deeper, not to climb out. Rationally, it is better to resolve moral issues without making more controversial assumptions than are needed. The question of who has inherent value is such a question, one that is resolved more rationally without the introduction of the idea of immortal souls than by its use.

Well, perhaps some will say that animals have some inherent value, only less than we have. Once again, however, attempts to defend this view can be shown to lack rational justification. What could be the basis of our having more inherent value than animals? Their lack of reason, or autonomy, or intellect? Only if we are willing to make the same judgment in the case of humans who are similarly deficient. But it is not true that such humans—the retarded child, for example, or the mentally deranged—have less inherent value than you or I. Neither, then, can we rationally sustain the view that animals, like them in being the experiencing subjects of a life, have less inherent value. *All* who have inherent value have it *equally,* whether they be human animals or not.

Inherent value, then, belongs equally to those who are the experiencing subjects of a life. Whether it belongs to others—to rocks and rivers, trees and glaciers, for example—we do not know and may never know. But neither do we need to know, if we are to make the case for animal rights. We do not need to know, for example, how many people are eligible to vote in the next presidential election before we can know whether I am. Similarly, we do not need to know how many individuals have inherent value before we can know that some do. When it comes to the case for animal rights, then, what we need to know is whether the animals that, in our culture, are routinely eaten, hunted and used in our laboratories, for example, are like us in being subjects of a life. And we do know this. We do know that many—literally, billions and billions—of these animals are the subjects of a life in the sense explained and so have inherent value if we do. And since, in order to arrive at the best theory of our duties to one another, we must recognize our equal inherent value as individuals, reason—not sentiment, not emotion—reason compels us to recognize the equal inherent value of these animals and, with this, their equal right to be treated with respect.

That, *very* roughly, is the shape and feel of the case for animal rights.

Most of the details of the supporting argument are missing. They are to be found in the book to which I alluded earlier. Here, the details go begging, and I must, in closing, limit myself to four final points.

The first is how the theory that underlies the case for animal rights shows that the animal rights movement is a part of, not antagonistic to, the human rights movement. The theory that rationally grounds the rights of animals also grounds the rights of humans. Thus those involved in the animal rights movement are partners in the struggle to secure respect for human rights—the rights of women, for example, or minorities, or workers. The animal rights movement is cut from the same moral cloth as these.

Second, having set out the broad outlines of the rights view, I can now say why its implications for . . . science, among other fields, are both clear and uncompromising. In the case of the use of animals in science, the rights view is categorically abolitionist. Lab animals are not our tasters; we are not their kings. Because these animals are treated routinely, systematically as if their value were reducible to their usefulness to others, they are routinely, systematically treated with a lack of respect, and thus are their rights routinely, systematically violated. This is just as true when they are used in trivial, duplicative, unnecessary or unwise research as it is when they are used in studies that hold out real promise of human benefits. We can't justify harming or killing a human being (my Aunt Bea, for example) just for these sorts of reason. Neither can we do so even in the case of so lowly a creature as a laboratory rat. It is not just refinement or reduction that is called for, not just larger, cleaner cages, not just more generous use of anesthetic or the elimination of multiple surgery, not just tidying up the system. It is complete replacement. The best we can do when it comes to using animals in science is—not to use them. That is where our duty lies, according to the rights view. . . .

My last two points are about philosophy, my profession. It is, most obviously, no substitute for political action. The words I have written here and in other places by themselves don't change a thing. It is what we do with the thoughts that the words express—our acts, our deeds—that changes things. All that philosophy can do, and all I have attempted, is to offer a vision of what our deeds should aim at. And the why. But not the how.

Finally, I am reminded of my thoughtful critic, the one I mentioned earlier, who chastised me for being too cerebral. Well, cerebral I have been: indirect duty views, utilitarianism, contractarianism—hardly the stuff deep passions are made of. I am also reminded, however, of the image another friend once set before me—the image of the ballerina as expressive of disciplined passion. Long hours of sweat and toil, of loneliness and practice, of doubt and fatigue: those are the discipline of her craft. But the passion is there too, the fierce drive to excel, to speak through her body, to do it right, to pierce our minds. That is the image of philosophy I would leave with you, not "too cerebral" but *disciplined passion.* Of the discipline enough has been seen. As for the passion: there are times, and these not infrequent, when tears come to my eyes when I see, or read, or hear of the wretched plight of animals in the hands of humans. Their pain, their suffering, their loneliness, their innocence, their death. Anger. Rage. Pity. Sorrow. Disgust. The whole creation groans under the weight of the evil we humans visit upon these mute, powerless creatures. It *is* our hearts, not just our heads, that call for an end to it all, that demand of us that we overcome, for them, the habits and forces behind their systematic oppression. All great movements, it is written, go through three stages: ridicule, discussion, adoption. It is the realization of this third stage, adoption, that requires both our passion and our discipline, our hearts and our heads. The fate of animals is in our hands. God grant we are equal to the task.

9

Difficulties with the Strong Animal Rights Position

Mary Anne Warren

Tom Regan has produced what is perhaps the definitive defense of the view that the basic moral rights of at least some non-human animals are in no way inferior to our own. In *The Case for Animal Rights,* he argues that all normal mammals over a year of age have the same basic moral rights.[1] Non-human mammals have essentially the same right not to be harmed or killed as we do. I shall call this "the strong animal rights position," although it is weaker than the claims made by some animal liberationists in that it ascribes rights to only some sentient animals.[2]

I will argue that Regan's case for the strong animal rights position is unpersuasive and that this position entails consequences which a reasonable person cannot accept. I do not deny that some non-human animals have moral rights; indeed, I would extend the scope of the rights claim to include all sentient animals, that is, all those capable of having experiences, including experiences of pleasure or satisfaction and pain, suffering, or frustration.[3] However, I do not think that the moral rights of most non-human animals are identical in strength to those of persons.[4] The rights of most non-human animals may be overridden in circumstances

From *Between the Species* 2, no. 4 (Fall 1987):163–73. Reprinted by permission of the author and the publisher.

which would not justify overriding the rights of persons. There are, for instance, compelling realities which sometimes require that we kill animals for reasons which could not justify the killing of persons. I will call this view "the weak animal rights" position, even though it ascribes rights to a wider range of animals than does the strong animal rights position.

I will begin by summarizing Regan's case for the strong animal rights position and noting two problems with it. Next, I will explore some consequences of the strong animal rights position which I think are unacceptable. Finally, I will outline the case for the weak animal rights position.

REGAN'S CASE

Regan's argument moves through three stages. First, he argues that normal, mature mammals are not only sentient but have other mental capacities, as well. These include the capacities for emotion, memory, belief, desire, the use of general concepts, intentional action, a sense of the future, and some degree of self-awareness. Creatures with such capacities are said to be subjects-of-a-life. They are not only alive in the biological sense but have a psychological identity over time and an existence which can go better or worse for them. Thus, they can be harmed or benefitted. These are plausible claims, and well defended. One of the strongest parts of the book is the rebuttal of philosophers, such as R. G. Frey, who object to the application of such mentalistic terms to creatures that do not use a human-style language.[5] The second and third stages of the argument are more problematic.

In the second stage, Regan argues that subjects-of-a-life have inherent value. His concept of inherent value grows out of his opposition to utilitarianism. Utilitarian moral theory, he says, treats individuals as "mere receptacles" for morally significant value, in that harm to one individual may be justified by the production of a greater net benefit to other individuals. In opposition to this, he holds that subjects-of-a-life have a value independent of both the value they may place upon their lives or experiences and the value others may place upon them.

Inherent value, Regan argues, does not come in degrees. To hold that some individuals have more inherent value than others is to adopt a "perfectionist" theory, i.e., one which assigns different moral worth to individuals according to how well they are thought to exemplify some virtue(s), such as intelligence or moral autonomy. Perfectionist theories have been used, at least since the time of Aristotle, to rationalize such injustices as slavery and male domination, as well as the unrestrained exploitation of animals. Regan argues that if we reject these injustices, then we must also reject perfectionism and conclude that all subjects-of-a-life have equal inherent value. Moral agents have no more inherent value than moral patients, i.e., subjects-of-a-life who are not morally responsible for their actions.

In the third phase of the argument, Regan uses the thesis of equal inherent value to derive strong moral rights for all subjects-of-a-life. This thesis underlies the Respect Principle, which forbids us to treat beings who have inherent value as mere receptacles, i.e., mere means to the production of the greatest overall good. This principle, in turn, underlies the Harm Principle, which says that we have a direct *prima facie* duty not to harm beings who have inherent value. Together, these principles give rise to moral rights. Rights are defined as valid claims, claims to certain goods and against certain beings, i.e., moral agents. Moral rights generate duties not only to refrain from inflicting harm upon beings with inherent value but also to come to their aid when they are threatened by other moral agents. Rights are not absolute but may be overridden in certain circumstances. Just what these circumstances are we will consider later. But first, let's look at some difficulties in the theory as thus far presented.

THE MYSTERY OF INHERENT VALUE

Inherent value is a key concept in Regan's theory. It is the bridge between the plausible claim that all normal, mature mammals—human or otherwise—are subjects-of-a-life and the more debatable claim that they all have basic moral rights of the same strength. But it is a highly obscure concept, and its obscurity makes it ill-suited to play this crucial role.

Inherent value is defined almost entirely in negative terms. It is not dependent upon the value which either the inherently valuable individual or anyone else may place upon that individual's life or experiences. It is not (necessarily) a function of sentience or any other mental capacity, because, Regan says, some entities which are not sentient (e.g., trees, rivers, or rocks) may, nevertheless, have inherent value (p. 246). It cannot attach to anything other than an individual; species, eco-systems, and the like cannot have inherent value.

These are some of the things which inherent value is not. But what is it? Unfortunately, we are not told. Inherent value appears as a mysterious non-natural property which we must take on faith. Regan says that it is a *postulate* that subjects-of-a-life have inherent value, a postulate justified by the fact that it avoids certain absurdities which he thinks follow from a purely utilitarian theory (p. 247). But why is the postulate that *subjects-of-a-life* have inherent value? If the inherent value of a being is completely independent of the value that it or anyone else places upon its experiences, then why does the fact that it has certain sorts of experiences constitute evidence that it has inherent value? If the reason is that subjects-of-a-life have an existence which can go better or worse for them, then why isn't the appropriate conclusion that all sentient beings have inherent value, since they would all seem to meet that condition? Sentient but mentally unsophisticated beings may have a less extensive range of possible satisfactions and frustrations, but why should it follow that they have—or may have—no inherent value at all?

In the absence of a positive account of inherent value, it is also difficult to grasp the connection between being inherently valuable and having moral rights. Intuitively, it seems that value is one thing, and rights are another. It does not seem incoherent to say that some things (e.g., mountains, rivers, redwood trees) are inherently valuable and yet are not the sorts of things which can have moral rights. Nor does it seem incoherent to ascribe inherent value to some things which are not individuals, e.g., plant or animal species, though it may well be incoherent to ascribe moral rights to such things.

In short, the concept of inherent value seems to create at least as many problems as it solves. If inherent value is based on some natural property, then why not try to identify that property and explain its moral significance, without appealing to inherent value? And if it is not based on any natural property, then why should we believe in it? That it may enable us to avoid some of the problems faced by the utilitarian is not a sufficient reason, if it creates other problems which are just as serious.

IS THERE A SHARP LINE?

Perhaps the most serious problems are those that arise when we try to apply the strong animal rights position to animals other than normal, mature mammals. Regan's theory requires us to divide all living things into two categories: those which have the same inherent value and the same basic moral rights that we do, and those which have no inherent value and presumably no moral rights. But wherever we try to draw the line, such a sharp division is implausible.

It would surely be arbitrary to draw such a sharp line between normal, mature mammals and all other living things. Some birds (e.g., crows, magpies, parrots, mynahs) appear to be just as mentally sophisticated as most mammals and thus are equally strong candidates for inclusion under the subject-of-a-life criterion. Regan is not in fact advocating that we draw the line here. His claim is only that normal, mature mammals are clear cases, while other cases are less clear. Yet, on his theory, there must be such a sharp line *somewhere,* since there are no degrees of inherent value. But why should we believe that there is a sharp line between creatures that are subjects-of-a-life and creatures that are not? Isn't it more likely that "subjecthood" comes in degrees, that some creatures have only a little self-awareness, and only a little capacity to anticipate the future, while some have a little more, and some a good deal more?

Should we, for instance, regard fish, amphibians, and reptiles as subjects-of-a-life? A simple yes-or-no answer seems inadequate. On the one hand, some of their behavior is difficult to explain without the assumption that they have sensations, beliefs, desires, emotions, and memories; on the other hand, they do not seem to exhibit very much self-awareness or very much conscious anticipation of future events. Do they have enough mental sophistication to count as subjects-of-a-life? Exactly how much is enough?

It is still more unclear what we should say about insects, spiders, octopi, and other invertebrate animals which have brains and sensory organs but whose minds (if they have minds) are even more alien to us than those of fish or reptiles. Such creatures are probably sentient. Some people doubt that they can feel pain, since they lack certain neurological structures which are crucial to the processing of pain impulses in vertebrate animals. But this argument is inconclusive, since their nervous systems might process pain in ways different from ours. When injured, they sometimes act as if they are in pain. On evolutionary grounds, it seems unlikely that highly mobile creatures with complex sensory systems would not have developed a capacity for pain (and pleasure), since such a capacity has obvious survival value. It must, however, be admitted that we do not *know* whether spiders can feel pain (or something very like it), let alone whether they have emotions, memories, beliefs, desires, self-awareness, or a sense of the future.

Even more mysterious are the mental capacities (if any) of mobile microfauna. The brisk and efficient way that paramecia move about in their incessant search for food *might* indicate some kind of sentience, in spite of their lack of eyes, ears, brains, and other organs associated with sentience in more complex organisms. It is conceivable—though not very probable—that they, too, are subjects-of-a-life.

The existence of a few unclear cases need not pose a serious problem for a moral theory, but in this case, the unclear cases constitute most of those with which an adequate theory of animal rights would need to deal. The subject-of-a-life criterion can provide us with little or no moral guidance in our interactions with the vast majority of animals. That might be acceptable if it could be supplemented with additional principles which would provide such guidance. However, the radical dualism of the theory precludes supplementing it in this way. We are forced to say that either a spider has the same right to life as you and I do, or it has no right to life whatever—and that only the gods know which of these alternatives is true.

Regan's suggestion for dealing with such unclear cases is to apply the "benefit of the doubt" principle. That is, when dealing with beings that may or may not be subjects-of-a-life, we should act as if they are.[6] But if we try to apply this principle to the entire range of doubtful cases, we will find ourselves with moral obligations which we cannot possibly fulfill. In many climates, it is virtually impossible to live without swatting mosquitoes and exterminating cockroaches, and not all of us can afford to hire someone to sweep the path before we walk, in order to make sure that we do not step on ants. Thus, we are still faced with the daunting task of drawing a sharp line somewhere on the continuum of life forms— this time, a line demarcating the limits of the benefit of the doubt principle.

The weak animal rights theory provides a more plausible way of dealing with this range of cases, in that it allows the rights of animals of different kinds to vary in strength. . . .

WHY ARE ANIMAL RIGHTS WEAKER THAN HUMAN RIGHTS?

How can we justify regarding the rights of persons as generally stronger than those of sentient beings which are not persons? There are a plethora of bad justifications, based on religious premises or false or unprovable claims about the differences between human and non-human nature. But there is one difference which has a clear moral relevance: people are at least sometimes capable of being moved to action or inaction by the force of reasoned argument. Rationality rests upon other mental capacities, notably those which Regan cites as criteria for being a subject-of-a-life. We share these capacities with many other animals. But it is not just because we are subjects-of-a-life that we are both able and morally compelled to recognize one another as beings with equal basic moral rights. It is also because we are able to "listen to reason" in order to settle our conflicts and cooperate in shared projects. This capacity, unlike the others, may require something like a human language.

Why is rationality morally relevant? It does not make us "better" than other animals or more "perfect." It does not even automatically make us more intelligent. (Bad reasoning reduces our effective intelligence rather than increasing it.) But it is morally relevant insofar as it provides greater possibilities for cooperation and for the nonviolent resolution of problems. It also makes us more dangerous than non-rational beings can ever be. Because we are potentially more dangerous and less predictable than wolves, we need an articulated system of morality to regulate our conduct. Any human morality, to be workable in the long run, must recognize the equal moral status of all persons, whether through the postulate of equal basic moral rights or in some other way. The recognition of the moral equality of other persons is the price we must each pay for their recognition of our moral equality. Without this mutual recognition of moral equality, human society can exist only in a state of chronic and bitter conflict. The war between the sexes will persist so long as there is sexism and male domination; racial conflict will never be eliminated so long as there are racist laws and practices. But, to the extent that we achieve a mutual recognition of equality, we can hope to live together, perhaps as peacefully as wolves, achieving (in part) through explicit moral principles what they do not seem to need explicit moral principles to achieve.

Why not extend this recognition of moral equality to other creatures, even though they cannot do the same for us? The answer is that we cannot. Because we cannot reason with most non-human animals, we cannot always solve the problems which they may cause without harming them—although we are always obligated to try. We cannot negotiate a treaty with the feral cats and foxes, requiring them to stop preying on endangered native species in return for suitable concessions on our part.

If rats invade our houses . . . we cannot reason with them, hoping to persuade them of the injustice they do us. We can only attempt to get rid
of them.[7]

Aristotle was not wrong in claiming that the capacity to alter one's
behavior on the basis of reasoned argument is relevant to the full moral
status which he accorded to free men. Of course, he was wrong in his
other premise, that women and slaves by their nature cannot reason well
enough to function as autonomous moral agents. Had that premise been
true, so would his conclusion that women and slaves are not quite the
moral equals of free men. In the case of most non-human animals, the
corresponding premise is true. If, on the other hand, there are animals
with whom we can (learn to) reason, then we are obligated to do this
and to regard them as our moral equals.

Thus, to distinguish between the rights of persons and those of most
other animals on the grounds that only people can alter their behavior
on the basis of reasoned argument does not commit us to a perfectionist
theory of the sort Aristotle endorsed. There is no excuse for refusing to
recognize the moral equality of some people on the grounds that we don't
regard them as quite as rational as we are, since it is perfectly clear that
most people can reason well enough to determine how to act so as to
respect the basic rights of others (if they choose to), and that is enough
for moral equality.

But what about people who are clearly not rational? It is often argued that sophisticated mental capacities such as rationality cannot be
essential for the possession of equal basic moral rights, since nearly everyone agrees that human infants and mentally incompetent persons have
such rights, even though they may lack those sophisticated mental capacities. But this argument is inconclusive, because there are powerful practical and emotional reasons for protecting non-rational human beings,
reasons which are absent in the case of most non-human animals. Infancy
and mental incompetence are human conditions which all of us either
have experienced or are likely to experience at some time. We also protect babies and mentally incompetent people because we care for them.
We don't normally care for animals in the same way, and when we do—
e.g., in the case of much-loved pets—we may regard them as having special
rights by virtue of their relationship to us. We protect them not only for
their sake but also for our own, lest we be hurt by harm done to them.
Regan holds that such "side-effects" are irrelevant to moral rights, and

perhaps they are. But in ordinary usage, there is no sharp line between moral rights and those moral protections which are not rights. The extension of strong moral protections to infants and the mentally impaired in no way proves that non-human animals have the same basic moral rights as people.

WHY SPEAK OF "ANIMAL RIGHTS" AT ALL?

If, as I have argued, reality precludes our treating all animals as our moral equals, then why should we still ascribe rights to them? Everyone agrees that animals are entitled to some protection against human abuse, but why speak of animal *rights* if we are not prepared to accept most animals as our moral equals? The weak animal rights position may seem an unstable compromise between the bold claim that animals have the same basic moral rights that we do and the more common view that animals have no rights at all.

It is probably impossible to either prove or disprove the thesis that animals have moral rights by producing an analysis of the concept of a moral right and checking to see if some or all animals satisfy the conditions for having rights. The concept of a moral right is complex, and it is not clear which of its strands are essential. Paradigm rights holders, i.e., mature and mentally competent persons, are *both* rational and morally autonomous beings and sentient subjects-of-a-life. Opponents of animal rights claim that rationality and moral autonomy are essential for the possession of rights, while defenders of animal rights claim that they are not. The ordinary concept of a moral right is probably not precise enough to enable us to determine who is right on purely definitional grounds.

If logical analysis will not answer the question of whether animals have moral rights, practical considerations may, nevertheless, incline us to say that they do. The most plausible alternative to the view that animals have moral rights is that, while they do not have *rights,* we are, nevertheless, obligated not to be cruel to them. Regan argues persuasively that the injunction to avoid being cruel to animals is inadequate to express our obligations towards animals, because it focuses on the mental states of those who cause animal suffering, rather than on the harm done to the animals themselves (p. 158). Cruelty is inflicting pain or suffering and either taking pleasure in that pain or suffering or being more or less indifferent to it. Thus, to express the demand for the decent treatment of animals in terms of the rejection of cruelty is to invite the too easy response that those who subject animals to suffering are not being cruel because they regret the suffering they cause but sincerely believe that what they do is justified. The injunction to avoid cruelty is also inadequate in that it does not preclude the killing of animals—for any reason, however trivial—so long as it is done relatively painlessly.

The inadequacy of the anti-cruelty view provides one practical reason for speaking of animal rights. Another practical reason is that this is an age in which nearly all significant moral claims tend to be expressed in terms of rights. Thus, the denial that animals have rights, however carefully qualified, is likely to be taken to mean that we may do whatever we like to them, provided that we do not violate any human rights. In such a context, speaking of the rights of animals may be the only way to persuade many people to take seriously protests against the abuse of animals.

Why not extend this line of argument and speak of the rights of trees, mountains, oceans, or anything else which we may wish to see protected from destruction? Some environmentalists have not hesitated to speak in this way, and, given the importance of protecting such elements of the natural world, they cannot be blamed for using this rhetorical device. But, I would argue that moral rights can meaningfully be ascribed only to entities which have some capacity for sentience. This is because moral rights are protections designed to protect rights holders from harms or to provide them with benefits which matter *to them*. Only beings capable of sentience can be harmed or benefitted in ways which matter to them, for only such beings can like or dislike what happens to them or prefer some conditions to others. Thus, sentient animals, unlike mountains, rivers, or species, are at least logically possible candidates for moral rights. This fact, together with the need to end current abuses of animals—e.g., in scientific research . . . —provides a plausible case for speaking of animal rights.

CONCLUSION

I have argued that Regan's case for ascribing strong moral rights to all normal, mature mammals is unpersuasive because (1) it rests upon the obscure concept of inherent value, which is defined only in negative terms, and (2) it seems to preclude any plausible answer to questions about the moral status of the vast majority of sentient animals. . . .

The weak animal rights theory asserts that (1) any creature whose natural mode of life includes the pursuit of certain satisfactions has the right not to be forced to exist without the opportunity to pursue those satisfactions; (2) that any creature which is capable of pain, suffering, or frustration has the right that such experiences not be deliberately inflicted upon it without some compelling reason; and (3) that no sentient being should be killed without good reason. However, moral rights are not an all-or-nothing affair. The strength of the reasons required to override the rights of a non-human organism varies, depending upon—among other things—the probability that it is sentient and (if it is clearly sentient) its probable degree of mental sophistication. . . .

NOTES

1. Tom Regan, *The Case for Animal Rights* (Berkeley: University of California Press, 1983). All page references are to this edition.
2. For instance, Peter Singer, although he does not like to speak of rights, includes all sentient beings under the protection of his basic utilitarian principle of equal respect for like interests. (*Animal Liberation* [New York: Avon Books, 1975], p. 3.)
3. The capacity for sentience, like all of the mental capacities mentioned in what follows, is a disposition. Dispositions do not disappear whenever they are not currently manifested. Thus, sleeping or temporarily unconscious persons or non-human animals are still sentient in the relevant sense (i.e., still capable of sentience), so long as they still have the neurological mechanisms necessary for the occurrence of experiences.
4. It is possible, perhaps probable that some non-human animals—such as cetaceans and anthropoid apes—should be regarded as persons. If so, then the weak animal rights position holds that these animals have the same basic moral rights as human persons.
5. See R. G. Frey, *Interests and Rights: The Case Against Animals* (Oxford: Oxford University Press, 1980).
6. See, for instance, p. 319, where Regan appeals to the benefit of the doubt principle when dealing with infanticide and late-term abortion.
7. Bonnie Steinbock, "Speciesism and the Idea of Equality," *Philosophy* 53 (1978): 253.

Part Three

Supporters of
Animal Experimentation

10

The Case for the Use of Animals in Biomedical Research

Carl Cohen

Using animals as research subjects in medical investigations is widely condemned on two grounds: first, because it wrongly violates the *rights* of animals,[1] and second, because it wrongly imposes on sentient creatures much avoidable *suffering*.[2] Neither of these arguments is sound. The first relies on a mistaken understanding of rights; the second relies on a mistaken calculation of consequences. Both deserve definitive dismissal.

WHY ANIMALS HAVE NO RIGHTS

A right, properly understood, is a claim, or potential claim, that one party may exercise against another. The target against whom such a claim may be registered can be a single person, a group, a community, or (perhaps) all humankind. The content of rights claims also varies greatly: repayment of loans, nondiscrimination by employers, noninterference by the state, and so on. To comprehend any genuine right fully, therefore, we must know *who* holds the right, *against whom* it is held, and *to what* it is a right.

From *The New England Journal of Medicine* 315, no. 14 (October 2, 1986):865–69. Reprinted by permission of the publisher.

Alternative sources of rights add complexity. Some rights are grounded in constitution and law (e.g., the right of an accused to trial by jury); some rights are moral but give no legal claims (e.g., my right to your keeping the promise you gave me); and some rights (e.g., against theft or assault) are rooted both in morals and in law.

The differing targets, contents, and sources of rights, and their inevitable conflict, together weave a tangled web. Notwithstanding all such complications, this much is clear about rights in general: they are in every case claims, or potential claims, within a community of moral agents. Rights arise, and can be intelligibly defended, only among beings who actually do, or can, make moral claims against one another. Whatever else rights may be, therefore, they are necessarily human; their possessors are persons, human beings.

The attributes of human beings from which this moral capability arises have been described variously by philosophers, both ancient and modern: the inner consciousness of a free will (Saint Augustine)[3]; the grasp, by human reason, of the binding character of moral law (Saint Thomas)[4]; the self-conscious participation of human beings in an objective ethical order (Hegel)[5]; human membership in an organic moral community (Bradley)[6]; the development of the human self through the consciousness of other moral selves (Mead)[7]; and the underivative, intuitive cognition of the rightness of an action (Prichard).[8] Most influential has been Immanuel Kant's emphasis on the universal human possession of a uniquely moral will and the autonomy its use entails.[9] Humans confront choices that are purely moral; humans—but certainly not dogs or mice—lay down moral laws, for others and for themselves. Human beings are self-legislative, morally *auto-nomous*.

Animals (that is, nonhuman animals, the ordinary sense of that word) lack this capacity for free moral judgment. They are not beings of a kind capable of exercising or responding to moral claims. Animals therefore have no rights, and they can have none. This is the core of the argument about the alleged rights of animals. The holders of rights must have the capacity to comprehend rules of duty, governing all including themselves. In applying such rules, the holders of rights must recognize possible conflicts between what is in their own interest and what is just. Only in a community of beings capable of self-restricting moral judgments can the concept of a right be correctly invoked.

Humans have such moral capacities. They are in this sense self-legislative, are members of communities governed by moral rules, and do possess rights. Animals do not have such moral capacities. They are not morally self-legislative, cannot possibly be members of a truly moral community, and therefore cannot possess rights. In conducting research on animal subjects, therefore, we do not violate their rights, because they have none to violate.

To animate life, even in its simplest forms, we give a certain natural reverence. But the possession of rights presupposes a moral status not attained by the vast majority of living things. We must not infer, therefore, that a live being has, simply in being alive, a "right" to its life. The assertion that all animals, only because they are alive and have interests, also possess the "right to life"[10] is an abuse of that phrase, and wholly without warrant.

It does not follow from this, however, that we are morally free to do anything we please to animals. Certainly not. In our dealings with animals, as in our dealings with other human beings, we have obligations that do not arise from claims against us based on rights. Rights entail obligations, but many of the things one ought to do are in no way tied to another's entitlement. Rights and obligations are not reciprocals of one another, and it is a serious mistake to suppose that they are.

Illustrations are helpful. Obligations may arise from internal commitments made: physicians have obligations to their patients not grounded merely in their patients' rights. Teachers have such obligations to their students, shepherds to their dogs, and cowboys to their horses. Obligations may arise from differences of status: adults owe special care when playing with young children, and children owe special care when playing with young pets. Obligations may arise from special relationships: the payment of my son's college tuition is something to which he may have no right, although it may be my obligation to bear the burden if I reasonably can; my dog has no right to daily exercise and veterinary care, but I do have the obligation to provide these things for her. Obligations may arise from particular acts or circumstances: one may be obliged to another for a special kindness done, or obliged to put an animal out of its misery in view of its condition—although neither the human benefactor nor the dying animal may have had a claim of right.

Plainly, the grounds of our obligations to humans and to animals are manifold and cannot be formulated simply. Some hold that there is a general obligation to do no gratuitous harm to sentient creatures (the principle of nonmaleficence); some hold that there is a general obligation to do good to sentient creatures when that is reasonably within one's power (the principle of beneficence). In our dealings with animals, few will deny that we are at least obliged to act humanely—that is, to treat them with the decency and concern that we owe, as sensitive human beings, to other sentient creatures. To treat animals humanely, however, is not to treat them as humans or as the holders of rights.

A common objection, which deserves a response, may be paraphrased as follows:

> If having rights requires being able to make moral claims, to grasp and apply moral laws, then many humans—the brain-damaged, the comatose, the senile—who plainly lack those capacities must be without rights. But that is absurd. This proves [the critic concludes] that rights do not depend on the presence of moral capacities.[11]

This objection fails; it mistakenly treats an essential feature of humanity as though it were a screen for sorting humans. The capacity for moral judgment that distinguishes humans from animals is not a test to be administered to human beings one by one. Persons who are unable, because of some disability, to perform the full moral functions natural to human beings are certainly not for that reason ejected from the moral community. The issue is one of kind. Humans are of such a kind that they may be the subject of experiments only with their voluntary consent. The choices they make freely must be respected. Animals are of such a kind that it is impossible for them, in principle, to give or withhold voluntary consent or to make a moral choice. What humans retain when disabled, animals have never had.

A second objection, also often made, may be paraphrased as follows:

> Capacities will not succeed in distinguishing humans from the other animals. Animals also reason; animals also communicate with one another; animals also care passionately for their young; animals also exhibit desires and preferences.[12] Features of moral relevance—rationality, interdependence, and love—are not exhibited uniquely by human beings. Therefore [this critic concludes], there can be no solid moral distinction between humans and other animals.[13]

This criticism misses the central point. It is not the ability to communicate or to reason, or dependence on one another, or care for the young, or the exhibition of preference, or any such behavior that marks the critical divide. Analogies between human families and those of monkeys, or between human communities and those of wolves, and the like, are entirely beside the point. Patterns of conduct are not at issue. Animals do indeed exhibit remarkable behavior at times. Conditioning, fear, instinct, and intelligence all contribute to species survival. Membership in a community of moral agents nevertheless remains impossible for them. Actors subject to moral judgment must be capable of grasping the generality of an ethical premise in a practical syllogism. Humans act immorally often enough, but only they—never wolves or monkeys—can discern, by applying some moral rule to the facts of a case, that a given act ought or ought not to be performed. The moral restraints imposed by humans on themselves are thus highly abstract and are often in conflict with the self-interest of the agent. Communal behavior among animals, even when most intelligent and most endearing, does not approach autonomous morality in this fundamental sense.

Genuinely moral acts have an internal as well as an external dimension. Thus, in law, an act can be criminal only when the guilty deed, the actus reus, is done with a guilty mind, mens rea. No animal can ever commit a crime; bringing animals to criminal trial is the mark of primitive ignorance. The claims of moral right are similarly inapplicable to them. Does a lion have a right to eat a baby zebra? Does a baby zebra have a right not to be eaten? Such questions, mistakenly invoking the concept of right where it does not belong, do not make good sense. Those who condemn biomedical research because it violates "animal rights" commit the same blunder.

IN DEFENSE OF "SPECIESISM"

Abandoning reliance on animal rights, some critics resort instead to animal sentience—their feelings of pain and distress. We ought to desist from the imposition of pain insofar as we can. Since all or nearly all experimentation on animals does impose pain and could be readily forgone, say these critics, it should be stopped. The ends sought may be worthy, but those ends do not justify imposing agonies on humans, and by animals the agonies are felt no less. The laboratory use of animals (these critics conclude) must therefore be ended—or at least very sharply curtailed.

Argument of this variety is essentially utilitarian, often expressly so;[14] it is based on the calculation of the net product, in pains and pleasures, resulting from experiments on animals. Jeremy Bentham, comparing horses and dogs with other sentient creatures, is thus commonly quoted: "The question is not, Can they reason? nor Can they talk? but, Can they suffer?"[15]

Animals certainly can suffer and surely ought not to be made to suffer needlessly. But in inferring, from these uncontroversial premises, that biomedical research causing animal distress is largely (or wholly) wrong, the critic commits two serious errors.

The first error is the assumption, often explicitly defended, that all sentient animals have equal moral standing. Between a dog and a human being, according to this view, there is no moral difference; hence the pains suffered by dogs must be weighed no differently from the pains suffered by humans. To deny such equality, according to this critic, is to give unjust preference to one species over another; it is "speciesism." The most influential statement of this moral equality of species was made by Peter Singer:

> The racist violates the principle of equality by giving greater weight to the interests of members of his own race when there is a clash between their interests and the interests of those of another race. The sexist violates the principle of equality by favoring the interests of his own sex. Similarly the speciesist allows the interests of his own species to override the greater interests of members of other species. The pattern is identical in each case.[16]

This argument is worse than unsound; it is atrocious. It draws an offensive moral conclusion from a deliberately devised verbal parallelism that is utterly specious. Racism has no rational ground whatever. Differing degrees of respect or concern for humans for no other reason than that they are members of different races is an injustice totally without foundation in the nature of the races themselves. Racists, even if acting on the basis of mistaken factual beliefs, do grave moral wrong precisely because there is no morally relevant distinction among the races. The supposition of such differences has led to outright horror. The same is true of the sexes, neither sex being entitled by right to greater respect or concern than the other. No dispute here.

Between species of animate life, however—between (for example) humans on the one hand and cats or rats on the other—the morally relevant differences are enormous, and almost universally appreciated. Humans engage in moral reflection; humans are morally autonomous; humans are members of moral communities, recognizing just claims against their own interest. Human beings do have rights; theirs is a moral status very different from that of cats or rats.

I am a speciesist. Speciesism is not merely plausible; it is essential for right conduct, because those who will not make the morally relevant distinctions among species are almost certain, in consequence, to misapprehend their true obligations. The analogy between speciesism and racism is insidious. Every sensitive moral judgment requires that the differing natures of the beings to whom obligations are owed be considered. If all forms of animate life—or vertebrate animal life?—must be treated equally, and if therefore in evaluating a research program the pains of a rodent count equally with the pains of a human, we are forced to conclude (1) that neither humans nor rodents possess rights, or (2) that rodents possess all the rights that humans possess. Both alternatives are absurd. Yet one or the other must be swallowed if the moral equality of all species is to be defended.

Humans owe to other humans a degree of moral regard that cannot be owed to animals. Some humans take on the obligation to support and heal others, both humans and animals, as a principal duty in their lives; the fulfillment of that duty may require the sacrifice of many animals. If biomedical investigators abandon the effective pursuit of their professional objectives because they are convinced that they may not do to animals what the service of humans requires, they will fail, objectively, to do their duty. Refusing to recognize the moral differences among species is a sure path to calamity. (The largest animal rights group in the country is People for the Ethical Treatment of Animals; its codirector, Ingrid Newkirk, calls research using animal subjects "fascism" and "supremacism." "Animal liberationists do not separate out the *human* animal," she says, "so there is no rational basis for saying that a human being has special rights. A rat is a pig is a dog is a boy. They're all mammals.")[17]

Those who claim to base their objection to the use of animals in biomedical research on their reckoning of the net pleasures and pains produced make a second error, equally grave. Even if it were true—as it is surely not—that the pains of all animate beings must be counted equally, a cogent utilitarian calculation requires that we weigh all the consequences of the use, and of the nonuse, of animals in laboratory research. Critics relying (however mistakenly) on animal rights may claim to ignore the beneficial results of such research, rights being trump cards to which interest and advantage must give way. But an argument that is explicitly framed in terms of interest and benefit for all over the long run must attend also to the disadvantageous consequences of not using animals in research, and to all the achievements attained and attainable only through their use. The sum of the benefits of their use is utterly beyond quantification. The elimination of horrible disease, the increase of longevity, the avoidance of great pain, the saving of lives, and the improvement of the quality of lives (for humans and for animals) achieved through research using animals is so incalculably great that the argument of these critics, systematically pursued, establishes not their conclusion but its reverse: to refrain from using animals in biomedical research is, on utilitarian grounds, morally wrong.

When balancing the pleasures and pains resulting from the use of animals in research, we must not fail to place on the scales the terrible pains that would have resulted, would be suffered now, and would long continue had animals not been used. Every disease eliminated, every vaccine developed, every method of pain relief devised, every surgical procedure invented, every prosthetic device implanted—indeed, virtually every modern medical therapy is due, in part or in whole, to experimentation using animals. Nor may we ignore, in the balancing process, the predictable gains in human (and animal) well-being that are probably achievable in the future but that will not be achieved if the decision is made now to desist from such research or to curtail it.

Medical investigators are seldom insensitive to the distress their work may cause animal subjects. Opponents of research using animals are frequently insensitive to the cruelty of the results of the restrictions they would impose.[18] Untold numbers of human beings—real persons, although not now identifiable—would suffer grievously as the consequence of this well-meaning but shortsighted tenderness. If the morally relevant differences between humans and animals are borne in mind, and if all relevant considerations are weighed, the calculation of long-term consequences must give overwhelming support for biomedical research using animals.

CONCLUDING REMARKS

Substitution

The humane treatment of animals requires that we desist from experimenting on them if we can accomplish the same result using alternative methods —in vitro experimentation, computer simulation, or others. Critics of some experiments using animals rightly make this point.

It would be a serious error to suppose, however, that alternative techniques could soon be used in most research now using live animal subjects. No other methods now on the horizon—or perhaps ever to be available—can fully replace the testing of a drug, a procedure, or a vaccine, in live organisms. The flood of new medical possibilities being opened by the successes of recombinant DNA technology will turn to a trickle if testing on live animals is forbidden. When initial trials entail great risks, there may be no forward movement whatever without the use of live animal subjects. In seeking knowledge that may prove critical in later clinical applications, the unavailability of animals for inquiry may spell complete stymie. In the United States, federal regulations require the testing of new drugs and other products on animals, for efficacy and safety, before human beings are exposed to them.[19] We would not want it otherwise.

Every advance in medicine—every new drug, new operation, new therapy of any kind—must sooner or later be tried on a living being for the first time. That trial, controlled or uncontrolled, will be an experiment. The subject of that experiment, if it is not an animal, will be a human being. Prohibiting the use of live animals in biomedical research, therefore, or sharply restricting it, must result either in the blockage of much valuable research or in the replacement of animal subjects with human subjects. These are the consequences—unacceptable to most reasonable persons—of not using animals in research.

Reduction

Should we not at least reduce the use of animals in biomedical research? No, we should increase it, to avoid when feasible the use of humans as experimental subjects. Medical investigations putting human subjects at some risk are numerous and greatly varied. The risks run in such experiments are usually unavoidable, and (thanks to earlier experiments on animals) most such risks are minimal or moderate. But some experimental risks are substantial.

When an experimental protocol that entails substantial risk to humans comes before an institutional review board, what response is appropriate? The investigation, we may suppose, is promising and deserves support, so long as its human subjects are protected against unnecessary dangers. May not the investigators be fairly asked, Have you done all that you can to eliminate risk to humans by the extensive testing of that drug, that procedure, or that device on animals? To achieve maximal safety for humans we are right to require thorough experimentation on animal subjects before humans are involved.

Opportunities to increase human safety in this way are commonly missed; trials in which risks may be shifted from humans to animals are often not devised, sometimes not even considered. Why? For the investigator, the use of animals as subjects is often more expensive, in money and time, than the use of human subjects. Access to suitable human subjects is often quick and convenient, whereas access to appropriate animal subjects may be awkward, costly, and burdened with red tape. Physician-investigators have often had more experience working with human beings and know precisely where the needed pool of subjects is to be found and how they may be enlisted. Animals, and the procedures for their use, are often less familiar to these investigators. Moreover, the use of animals in place of humans is now more likely to be the target of zealous protests from without. The upshot is that humans are sometimes subjected to risks that animals could have borne, and should have borne, in their place. To maximize the protection of human subjects, I conclude, the wide and imaginative use of live animal subjects should be encouraged rather than discouraged. This enlargement in the use of animals is our obligation.

Consistency

Finally, inconsistency between the profession and the practice of many who oppose research using animals deserves comment. This frankly ad hominem observation aims chiefly to show that a coherent position rejecting the use of animals in medical research imposes costs so high as to be intolerable even to the critics themselves.

One cannot coherently object to the killing of animals in biomedical investigations while continuing to eat them. Anesthetics and thoughtful animal husbandry render the level of actual animal distress in the laboratory generally lower than that in the abattoir. So long as death and discomfort do not substantially differ in the two contexts, the consistent objector must not only refrain from all eating of animals but also protest as vehemently against others eating them as against others experimenting on them. No less vigorously must the critic object to the wearing of animal hides in coats and shoes, to employment in any industrial enterprise that uses animal parts, and to any commercial development that will cause death or distress to animals.

Killing animals to meet human needs for food, clothing, and shelter is judged entirely reasonable by most persons. The ubiquity of these uses and the virtual universality of moral support for them confront the opponent of research using animals with an inescapable difficulty. How can the many common uses of animals be judged morally worthy, while their use in scientific investigation is judged unworthy?

The number of animals used in research is but the tiniest fraction of the total used to satisfy assorted human appetites. That these appetites, often base and satisfiable in other ways, morally justify the far larger consumption of animals, whereas the quest for improved human health and understanding cannot justify the far smaller, is wholly implausible. Aside from the numbers of animals involved, the distinction in terms of worthiness of use, drawn with regard to any single animal, is not defensible. A given sheep is surely not more justifiably used to put lamb chops on the supermarket counter than to serve in testing a new contraceptive or a new prosthetic device. The needless killing of animals is wrong; if the common killing of them for our food or convenience is right, the less common but more humane uses of animals in the service of medical science are certainly not less right.

Scrupulous vegetarianism, in matters of food, clothing, shelter, commerce, and recreation, and in all other spheres, is the only fully coherent position the critic may adopt. At great human cost, the lives of fish and crustaceans must also be protected, with equal vigor, if speciesism has been forsworn. A very few consistent critics adopt this position. It is the reductio ad absurdum of the rejection of moral distinctions between animals and human beings.

Opposition to the use of animals in research is based on arguments of two different kinds—those relying on the alleged rights of animals and those relying on the consequences for animals. I have argued that arguments of both kinds must fail. We surely do have obligations to animals, but they have, and can have, no rights against us on which research can infringe. In calculating the consequences of animal research, we must weigh all the long-term benefits of the results achieved—to animals and to humans—and in that calculation we must not assume the moral equality of all animate species.

NOTES

1. T. Regan, *The Case for Animal Rights* (Berkeley, Calif.: University of California Press, 1983).
2. P. Singer, *Animal Liberation* (New York: Avon Books, 1977).
3. Augustine (A.D. 397), *Confessions* (New York: Pocketbooks, 1957), bk. 7, pp. 104–26.
4. Aquinas (A.D. 1273), *Summa Theologica* (Philosophic Texts) (New York: Oxford University Press, 1960), pp. 353–66.
5. G. W. F. Hegel (1821), *Philosophy of Right* (London: Oxford University Press, 1952), pp. 105–10.
6. F. H. Bradley, "Why Should I Be Moral?" in *Ethical Theories,* ed. A. I. Melden (New York: Prentice-Hall, 1950), pp. 345–59.
7. G. H. Mead (1925), "The Genesis of the Self and Social Control" in *Selected Writings,* ed. A. J. Reck (Indianapolis: Bobbs-Merrill, 1964), pp. 264–93.
8. H. A. Prichard (1912), "Does Moral Philosophy Rest on a Mistake?" in *Readings in Ethical Theory,* ed. W. Cellars and J. Hospers (New York: Appleton-Century-Crofts, 1952), pp. 149–63.
9. I. Kant (1785), *Fundamental Principles of the Metaphysic of Morals* (New York: Liberal Arts Press, 1949).
10. B. E. Rollin, *Animal Rights and Human Morality* (Buffalo, N.Y.: Prometheus Books, 1981).
11. [See note 1 and] C. Hoff, "Immoral and Moral Uses of Animals," *New England Journal of Medicine* 302 (1980): 115–18.
12. [See note 11 and] D. Jamieson, "Killing Persons and Other Beings," in *Ethics and Animals,* ed. H. B. Miller and W. H. Williams (Clifton, N.J.: Humana Press, 1983), pp. 135–46.
13. B. E. Rollin, *Animal Rights and Human Morality.*
14. P. Singer, "Ten Years of Animal Liberation," *New York Review of Books* 31 (1985): 46–52.
15. J. Bentham, *Introduction to the Principles of Morals and Legislation* (London: Athlone Press, 1970).
16. P. Singer, *Animal Liberation.*
17. K. McCabe, "Who Will Live, Who Will Die?" *Washingtonian Magazine,* August 1986, 115.
18. P. Singer, *Animal Liberation.*
19. U. S. Code of Federal Regulations, Title 21, Sect. 505(i). Food, Drug, and Cosmetic Regulations. U. S. Code of Federal Regulatons, Title 16, Sect. 1500.40–2. Consumer Product Regulations.

11

The Responsible Use of Animals in Biomedical Research

Edwin Converse Hettinger

Carl Cohen's defense of the use of animals for biomedical research in *The New England Journal of Medicine*[1] raises most of the major issues in the moral controversy concerning human treatment of nonhuman animals. It exhibits the major lines of attack against both animal rights advocates (such as Tom Regan)[2] and utilitarian animal-liberationists (such as Peter Singer).[3] It is also a showcase of the most common mistakes made by those who seek to defend the current human use of animals.

Cohen argues that although we do have obligations to animals—for example, not to be cruel to them—we have no obligations to animals based on their rights to such treatment. According to Cohen, the biomedical use of animals does not violate their rights, since by their very nature animals cannot have rights. Cohen rejects the utilitarian argument that much of the biomedical use of animals is an unjustified subordination of the most vital interests of animals to relatively minor human concerns. He thinks a proper utilitarian assessment of animal experimentation counsels the increased use of animals in biomedical research, rather than its reduction or elimination. Because there is a stronger justification for ani-

From *Between the Species* 5, no. 3 (Summer 1989):123–31. Reprinted by permission of the author and the publisher.

mal use in biomedical research than for any other use of animals (e.g., for food or clothing), Cohen argues that opponents of animal experimentation must adopt what he feels is the absurd position which opposes *all* use of animals.

In response, I argue that Cohen cannot secure the rights of severely retarded humans while denying that psychologically sophisticated animals have rights. Cohen can reach his conclusion that we should increase our biomedical use of animals only because (1) he counts animal pain and suffering as less important than equivalent human pain and suffering, (2) he ignores the frequent misuse of animals in biomedical research, and (3) he overlooks the abundant alternatives to current animal experimentation. I propose the limited use of animals based on their degree of psychological sophistication as a consistent and attractive alternative to the extreme views of both Cohen and his absolute prohibitionist opponents. I close by suggesting that only if researchers would be willing to experiment on severely retarded humans at comparable levels of psychological sophistication are their experiments on animals morally permissible.

DO ALL HUMANS BUT NO ANIMALS HAVE RIGHTS?

Cohen argues that only human beings can have rights.

> Rights arise, and can be intelligibly defended, only among beings who actually do, or can, make moral claims against one another. Whatever else rights may be, therefore, they are necessarily human; their possessors are persons, human beings. (p. 104)

Cohen is correct in maintaining that rights cannot arise unless there exist moral agents for whom these rights claims make sense. To say that some being has a right is to say (at least in part) that some other being has obligations to treat the right holder in certain ways specified by that right. So if there were no beings more cognitively and morally capable than pigs or dogs, there would be no rights.

However, the fact that rights claims require the existence of duty bearers does not imply that only those duty bearers can have rights. Even Cohen would grant that human infants have rights, yet they are not duty bearers. Thus, some creatures possess rights despite being unable to invoke them against others or to recognize and respect others' rights.

Cohen attempts to avoid this objection by shifting his criterion of rights possession to the *capacity* for being a moral agent, rather than actually being a moral agent.

> Animals . . . are not beings of a kind capable of exercising or responding to moral claims. Animals therefore have no rights, and they can have none . . . . The holders of rights must have the capacity to comprehend rules of duty . . . . (p. 104)

However, most people would grant that severely retarded humans have rights (Cohen does), and yet they do not have "the capacity to comprehend rules of duty." Thus if having the capacity to be a duty bearer is necessary for the possession of rights, then severely retarded humans cannot have rights.

Cohen responds to this point with his talk of "kinds."

> The capacity for moral judgment that distinguishes humans from animals is not a test to be administered to human beings one by one. Persons who are unable, because of some disability, to perform the full moral functions natural to human beings are certainly not for that reason ejected from the moral community. The issue is one of kind. Humans are of such a kind that they may be the subject of experiments only with their voluntary consent. The choices they make freely must be respected. Animals are of such a kind that it is impossible for them, in principle, to give or withhold voluntary consent or to make a moral choice. What humans retain when disabled, animals have never had. (p. 106)

Cohen seems to be claiming that the capacity for moral agency is essential to human beings and is necessarily lacking in other animals. Thus, severely retarded humans, because they are human, retain the capacity for moral agency even in their retarded state. Animals by their very nature lack this capacity. Since the capacity for moral agency confers rights, severely retarded humans have rights, whereas animals do not.

But many severely retarded humans could never carry out even the quasi-moral functions that some animals can perform. Dogs, for example, can be obedient, protective, and solicitous, while there are severely retarded humans who could not achieve these minimal moral abilities despite our best efforts. Given this fact, it just is not plausible to claim that severely retarded humans have the capacity for moral agency, while claiming that psychologically sophisticated animals do not. Cohen certainly has not given us any reason to accept this claim. He simply assumes that being a member of a biological species guarantees that one has certain capacities, despite overwhelming evidence that marginal members of species often lack capacities normal for that kind of creature. We need a strong argument before we should reject the obvious point that some animals have a greater capacity for moral behavior (however minimal) than do some severely retarded human beings.

Cohen might argue that severely retarded humans have the capacity for moral agency despite lacking the ability to realize that capacity. But why should we accept such an attenuated notion of capacity? Certainly capacities can be left unrealized, but if there is no possibility that they could ever be developed, what sense is there in claiming that the capacity is present? I see no reason to accept the notion that there can be unrealizable capacities.

IS SPECIESISM DEFENSIBLE?

Perhaps Cohen would agree that severely retarded humans lack the capacity for moral agency but thinks this is unimportant. He may be arguing that we should treat the severely retarded as human beings and that since human beings have rights (presumably because many of them are moral agents), severely retarded humans have rights as well. On this reading, Cohen is suggesting that we treat individuals according to their biological kind and ignore their individual characteristics. Moral status is to be determined by species membership, not individual qualities. This is "speciesism": the view that species membership is by itself a morally legitimate reason for treating individuals differently.

Peter Singer and others have argued that speciesism is "a form of prejudice no less objectionable than racism or sexism."[4] Cohen's speciesist perspective concerning the moral status of animals vis-a-vis humans does coincide uncomfortably with the outlook of racists and sexists toward blacks and women. Both judge according to class membership while ignoring individual qualities.

Cohen responds to this charge of speciesism by embracing it:

> I am a speciesist. Speciesism is not merely plausible; it is essential for right conduct, because those who will not make the morally relevant distinctions among species are almost certain, in consequence, to misapprehend their

true obligations. The analogy between speciesism and racism is insidious. Every sensitive moral judgment requires that the differing natures of the beings to whom obligations are owed be considered. (p. 109)

This passage defends the truism that there often are differences between members of distinct species which are morally relevant in determining how we should treat them. But this is not what is at issue in the debate over speciesism. Singer, Regan, and other opponents of speciesism are not suggesting that we ignore morally relevant differences between members of different species and treat them all identically. (They are not suggesting, for example, that dogs be allowed at the dinner table or be allowed to vote.) What rejecting speciesism commits one to is being unwilling to use difference in species by itself as a reason for treating individuals differently. Similarly, rejecting racism and sexism commits one to not using race or sex by itself as a reason for differential treatment. Cohen's truism does not support speciesism in this problematic sense.

The analogy between speciesism and racism or sexism is deficient in one respect. Species classification marks broader differences between beings than does racial or sexual classification. Thus attempting to justify differential treatment on the basis of species membership alone (as Cohen does) is not *just* as morally objectionable as doing so on the basis of race or sex, since members of different species are more likely to require differential treatment than are members of different races or sexes (within a species). For example, in determining what sort of food or shelter to provide, it would be much more important to know a creature's species than it would be to know a person's race or sex.

But this does not imply that difference in species by itself is a morally legitimate reason for treating individuals differently, while difference in race or sex considered by itself is not. Arguing that a woman should be prohibited from combat because of her sex fails to provide a morally relevant reason for the recommendation. Arguing for this on the grounds that this woman lacks the required physical capacities is to provide a morally relevant reason. Similarly, arguing that a chimpanzee should be experimentally sacrificed rather than a human, simply because it is a chimpanzee, gives no morally relevant reason for the recommendation. However, arguing that the chimpanzee does not value or plan for its future life to the extent that the human does is to provide such a reason.

Thus even though considerations of species are frequently more closely correlated with morally relevant features than are considerations of race or sex, species membership by itself (like racial or sexual class member-ship) is not a morally legitimate reason for differential treatment. Spe-ciesism is thus a moral mistake of the same sort as racism and sexism: it advocates differential treatment on morally illegitimate grounds.

The illegitimacy of judgments based on species membership alone becomes especially clear when comparing the moral status of a severely retarded human with that of psychologically sophisticated animals, since here the individual does not have what most members of the species have. The morally relevant differences which *usually* exist between individuals of two different biological kinds (and hence which would frequently justify treating them differently) are lacking when comparing severely retarded humans with psychologically sophisticated animals. Any plausible mor-ally relevant characteristic—whether it be rationality, self-sufficiency, abil-ity to communicate, free choice, moral agency, psychological sophistica-tion, fullness of life, and so on—is possessed by some animals to a greater extent than by some severely retarded humans. In this case, to classify by biological kind and to argue for differential treatment on that basis alone obscures and ignores morally relevant features rather than relying on them. We should not treat individuals on the basis of group or kind membership when their individual characteristics are readily apparent and relevant.

Thus, Cohen's argument fails on this second interpretation, as well. His appeal to biological kind to justify differential moral status of severely retarded humans and psychologically sophisticated animals is an unjustified form of speciesism. Unless Cohen can show us that there is some morally relevant difference between severely retarded humans and psychologically sophisticated animals, his position is open to the following objection: if experimenting on severely retarded humans is a violation of their rights, then experimenting on psychologically sophisticated animals violates their rights, as well.

DOES UTILITARIANISM JUSTIFY ANIMAL EXPERIMENTATION?

Utilitarians hold that the right policy is the one whose consequences maximize the satisfaction of interests. In this calculation the interests of all affected parties are fairly taken into account. Utilitarians who oppose animal experimentation do so not on the grounds that animal rights are violated but because they think that the overall good resulting from these experiments is not sufficient to justify their negative consequences. The benefits which result from animal experimentation (such as an increase in scientific and medical knowledge) either do not outweigh the costs (e.g., animal pain and death) or could be achieved in a less costly fashion.

Cohen rejects the utilitarian critic's position that the like interests of humans and animals should be given equal moral weight. He denies that similar amounts of human and animal pain are equally morally significant.

> The first error is the assumption, often explicitly defended, that all sentient animals have equal moral standing. Between a dog and a human being, according to this view, there is no moral difference; hence the pains suffered by dogs must be weighed no differently from the pains suffered by humans . . . . If all forms of animate life . . . must be treated equally, and if therefore in evaluating a research program the pains of a rodent count equally with the pains of a human, we are forced to conclude (1) that neither humans nor rodents possess rights, or (2) that rodents possess all the rights that humans possess . . . . One or the other must be swallowed if the moral equality of all species is to be defended. (pp. 108–9)

This argument misses the mark. To claim that animals "have equal moral standing" and should have their like interests treated equally implies neither that there are no moral differences between humans and animals nor that we should treat animals in the same manner that we do humans.

From the utilitarian position that the right act is the one which maximizes the net satisfaction of interests it follows that it is morally preferable to give a human a slightly less amount of pain than to give an animal a slightly greater amount of pain (or *vice versa*). If the pains are of equal intensity and consequence, then one should be morally indifferent. The fact that one is the pain of a human and the other is the pain of an animal is not by itself morally relevant.

This is not to say that the same type of experiment on a human and an animal would cause each the same amount of pain and suffering and that we should be indifferent to which being we use. Giving a typical chimpanzee a deadly virus in order to test a vaccine is likely to cause less pain and suffering than giving a typical human the deadly virus for the same purpose. The greater psychological sophistication of the human, its greater intelligence and self-consciousness, makes possible a greater degree of pain and suffering. (Sometimes the reverse is true, however.)[5]

Even though pain and suffering would often be minimized by experimenting on an animal instead of a typical human, that does not show that we may morally discount the pain and suffering of animals. We must still count the pain and suffering of animals equally with the like pain and suffering of humans. But in cases where a human will suffer more, we should prefer the use of animals (and *vice versa*).

Cohen is thus mistaken in thinking that giving equal consideration to the like interests of animals and humans makes moral discriminations between the two impossible. For a utilitarian, equal consideration (or equal moral standing) does not imply identical treatment. Cohen has given us no cogent reason for rejecting the view that the like pains of humans and animals must be given equal moral weight. Since the pain of the animals on whom we experiment cannot be discounted, Cohen's utilitarian justification for the biomedical use of animals becomes far more difficult to achieve.

Cohen argues that even if "the pains of all animate beings must be counted equally" (p. 109), a utilitarian calculus would still come out in support of the biomedical use of animals:

> The sum of the benefits of their use is utterly beyond quantification. The elimination of horrible disease, the increase of longevity, the avoidance of great pain, the saving of lives, and the improvement of the quality of lives (for humans and for animals) achieved through research using animals is so incalculably great that the argument of these critics, systematically pursued, establishes not their conclusion but its reverse: to refrain from using animals in biomedical research is, on utilitarian grounds, morally wrong. (p. 110)

Substantial benefits have resulted (and continue to result) from biomedical experimentation, much of which involves the use of animals. And although a utilitarian benefit/cost analysis would reach the conclusion that it would be wrong to stop the use of animals entirely, it would not justify Cohen's call for an increase in the biomedical use of animals. Cohen can reach this conclusion only by abandoning utilitarianism (and its principle of equal consideration of like interests), by adopting the speciesist position which treats animal pain and distress as insignificant when it is a means to human benefit, and by being overly pessimistic about the possibility of alternatives to animal use.

THE POSSIBILITY OF SUBSTITUTION

Whether research using living creatures is justified on utilitarian grounds depends in large part on the availability of substitute procedures. A utilitarian benefit/cost analysis (which must consider alternative, less costly ways to achieve these benefits) would find that some, perhaps many but certainly not all experiments, using animals are morally justifiable. *Some* use of living beings continues to be necessary and justifiable. Even developing alternatives to the biomedical use of animals often requires the use of animals. At present substitute techniques are not sufficiently developed to eliminate this use entirely (and they may never be).[6]

Nevertheless, Cohen is overly pessimistic about the possibility of alternatives to the current biomedical use of animals. His speciesism prevents him from appreciating or even acknowledging the numerous substitute procedures that are being developed. A recent report by the U.S. Congress' Office of Technology Assessment (OTA) on alternatives to animal use in research, testing, and education is much more encouraging about the potential for alternatives.[7] This study presents numerous suggestions involving the replacement, reduction, and refinement of the use of animals. In addition to the promising techniques of in vitro experimentation and computer simulation (which Cohen mentions), the OTA report suggests:

(1) Coordinating investigations and sharing information (to reduce duplicative experiments when necessary for validating the original research);

(2) Replacing the use of higher animals with lower animals (invertebrates for vertebrates and cold-blooded for warm-blooded animals);

(3) Using plants instead of animals;

(4) Sharing animals (e.g., getting several tissues from one animal);

(5) Designing experiments which use statistical inferences and whose design provides reliable information despite the use of fewer animals;

(6) Decreasing the pain and distress in animal experimentation by altering the experimental design and by using anesthetics and tranquilizers;

(7) Using non-living chemical and physical systems that mimic biological functions;

(8) Using human and animal cadavers; and

(9) Teaching by demonstration instead of by individual student use of animals.

Recent amendments to the Animal Welfare Act[8] and the Public Health Service Act,[9] as well as legislation concerning the education of health professionals,[10] all encourage alternatives to the current methods of animal use.[11] Cohen's pessimistic assessment of these alternatives flies in the face of a growing trend of using already existing alternatives and of developing new substitute procedures. Experiments which cause animals pain, distress, or death are clearly not justifiable when such substitute procedures are available.

SHOULD WE INCREASE BIOMEDICAL ANIMAL USE?

Cohen argues that in order to achieve maximum safety for humans "the wide and imaginative use of live animal subjects should be encouraged rather than discouraged" (p. 112). Cohen is right that some experiments which subject humans to risk could be conducted using animals without loss in the significance of the results. Furthermore, risky experiments which are necessary *should* be performed on psychologically less sophisticated creatures. An increase in psychological sophistication brings with it a wider range of interests, a greater ability to experience satisfaction (and dissatisfaction), and the possibility of leading a fuller life. Inflicting suffering or death on these creatures causes greater harm.

In advocating an increase in the biomedical use of animals Cohen not only ignores the available alternatives but disregards the widespread experimental misuse of animals, as well. Numerous books and articles have persuasively documented that many experiments using animals have been unprofessional, of dubious scientific merit, repetitive, or cruel.[12] Two video tapes are especially persuasive; "Unnecessary Fuss," about head injury research involving baboons at the University of Pennsylvania,[13] and "Tools for Research," a general review of research using animals over the last twenty years.[14] The flurry of recent legislation concerning animal welfare cited above shows a growing public recognition of the misuse of laboratory animals. Government regulations for the care of laboratory animals have been developed to prevent these sorts of experiments, as well.[15] Cohen's suggestion that we encourage the wide and imaginative use of live animal subjects, instead of limiting this use and working to find substitute techniques, shows blatant disregard for this widely acknowledged problem.

CAN A CONSISTENT POSITION CONCERNING
ANIMAL USE BE DEVELOPED?

Cohen charges his anti-speciesist opponents with inconsistency or absurdity: "Scrupulous vegetarianism, in matters of food, clothing , shelter, commerce, and recreation, and in all other spheres, is the only fully coherent position the critic may adopt" (p. 113). The person who eats veal and then strenuously objects to the killing of cats in relatively painless medical experiments *is* inconsistent. We do not *need* to eat animals for food (certainly not mammals); carefully chosen vegetarian diets are perfectly healthy. We do need the ongoing results of biomedical research, and for some of this research the use of living creatures continues to be required.

Cohen is right that the use of animals in biomedical research is less difficult to defend than are other uses of animals. (Only one out of every hundred animals used is for this purpose.)[16] But the anti-speciesist critic of current biomedical uses of animals need not be committed to prohibiting all uses of animals. Since anti-speciesism allows for discriminating between animals, critics can consistently object to the raising, slaughtering, and consumption of veal calves while not objecting to commercial shrimp farming and shrimp consumption. A critic might also object to repeated surgery on healthy animals in the training of veterinarians and not object to the use of chick embryos for toxicity testing. The recommendation that experimenters substitute cold-blooded animals for warm-blooded ones or invertebrates for vertebrates is also perfectly consistent. These suggestions are not speciesist, since species membership *per se* is not the justification offered for differential treatment. Differences in the fullness of life, in psychological sophistication, and in the capacity for suffering are what motivates these suggestions.

Thus, one can argue for limiting animal use in biomedical research without embracing the extreme position prohibiting all uses of any animals for whatever reason. Cohen can successfully saddle only his most extreme opponents with this consequence. A more circumspect skepticism about the legitimacy of a significant portion of laboratory animal use is possible. Advocates of limiting the use of animals in biomedical research can consistently advocate the limited use of animals in other areas, as well. Both extremes—the absolute prohibition of all animal use, as well as Cohen's speciesist encouragement of such use—should be avoided.

A TEST BIOMEDICAL RESEARCHERS SHOULD USE

I have suggested that it would be morally preferable, *ceteris paribus,* to give a deadly virus to an animal rather than to a typical human being. The pain, suffering, and distress caused by the two experiments, as well as the significance of the loss of life, would be minimized by experimenting on the animal. However, this argument in support of the experimental use of animals rather than typical humans does not give us a reason for preferring animal experimentation to "marginal case" human experimentation. Since many animals (e.g., chimpanzees) and *severely* retarded humans would suffer equally from such an experiment, the pain and distress of the experimental subject gives us no reason to prefer the use of one to the other. Furthermore, given their rough equivalence in psychological sophistication, the value of the two creatures' lives is about the same. Whatever moral rights such creatures have, if any, are also comparable.

Thus, an important test to determine if an experiment is significant enough to justify the pain, suffering, and (perhaps) death of the creature involved is to ask the following question: Would the investigator still think the experiment justifiable if it were performed on a severely retarded human at a comparable psychological level as the animal? If not, then the experiment should not be conducted. Only an arbitrary preference for members of our own species could avoid this conclusion.

If this test were used, and I am arguing that it is the appropriate test, many—though certainly not all—experiments on animals would cease and be replaced by alternatives. Biomedical researchers would do well to keep this test in mind.[17]

NOTES

1. Carl Cohen, "The Case for the Use of Animals in Biomedical Research," *New England Journal of Medicine* 315 (1986): 865–70. [All page references are to section 10 of this volume]

2. Tom Regan, *The Case for Animal Rights* (Berkeley, Calif.: University of California Press, 1983).

3. Peter Singer, *Animal Liberation* (New York: Avon Books, 1975).

4. Peter Singer, "Animal Liberation" in *People, Penguins, and Plastics,* ed. Donald VanDeVeer and Christine Pierce (Belmont, Calif.: Wadsworth, 1986), p. 31.

5. Peter Singer, *Practical Ethics* (Cambridge: Cambridge University Press, 1979), p. 53.

6. Office of Technology Assessment (OTA), *Alternatives to Animal Use in Research, Testing, and Education,* publication no. OTA-BA-273 (Washington, D.C.: U.S. Government Printing Office, 1986), p. 138.

7. Ibid

8. The Food Security Act of 1985 (Public Law 99–198).

9. The Health Research Extension Act of 1985 (Public Law 99–158).

10. The Health Professions Educational Assistance Amendments of 1985 (Public Law 99–129).

11. See OTA, *Alternatives to Animal Use in Research, Testing, and Education,* chap. 13.

12. See Singer, *Animal Liberation,* chap. 2; Richard Ryder, "Speciesism in the Laboratory" in *In Defense of Animals,* ed. Peter Singer (New York: Basil Blackwell, 1985) pp. 77–88; Dale Jamieson and Tom Regan, "On the Ethics of the Use of Animals in Science," in *And Justice For All* (Totowa, N.J.: Rowman and Littlefield, 1982), pp. 169–96; Bernard Rollin, *Animal Rights and Human Morality* (Buffalo, N.Y.: Prometheus Books, 1981), chap. 3.

13. Available from People for the Ethical Treatment of Animals, P.O. Box 42516, Washington, D.C. 20015.

14. Available from Bullfrog Films, Inc., Olney, Penn.

15. See National Institutes of Health, *Guidelines for the Care and Use of Laboratory Animals,* NIH publication no. 85–23 (Bethesda, Md.: National Institutes of Health, 1985).

16. See OTA, *Alternatives to Animal Use in Research, Testing, and Education,* p. 43.

17. I would like to thank Beverly Diamond, John Dickerson, Martin Perlmutter, and Hugh Wilder for helpful suggestions on earlier drafts of this paper.

12

Animal Pain

Peter Harrison

I

. . . In the seventeenth century Descartes proposed that animals were simply machines who were unaware of sensations of any kind—sights, sounds, smells, and crucially, pain.[1] Descartes did not, we should note, deny animals life, he denied them awareness. Animals, for him, were like trees which had developed the art of locomotion. . . . Descartes's speculations, however, were accompanied by serious difficulties. Notoriously, mind-body dualism, upon which his view of the nature of animals ultimately rests, gives rise to a number of paradoxes, the most serious of which concerns the interaction of mind and body. More than internal philosophical difficulties, however, it was the acceptance of evolutionary theory which led to the demise of the animal-machine. The evolutionary model, which stresses continuities between human and animal realms, displaced the quasi-religious Cartesian model with its emphasis on the immortal soul and on the privileged position of man in creation. . . .

. . . I wish to show that Descartes' view of animal pain . . . can seriously be entertained without the necessity of subscribing to Descartes's unfortunate ontology.

From "Theodicy and Animal Pain," *Philosophy* 64, no. 247 (January 1989): 79–92. Copyright © 1989. Reprinted by permission of the author and Cambridge University Press.

II

No strict argument can be mounted for or against the existence of animal pain. Indeed it is difficult to see what form such an argument might take, for it is the essence of pain that it is a private experience. Accordingly, my chief means of persuasion will be centered on our own experiences of pain, and the ways in which they might or might not be analogous to the experiences of animals in comparable situations. But first I will examine some of the reasons for our assumption that certain animals suffer pain in the way that we do.

The animal-machine model fell from favor at least in part because of the acceptance of an evolutionary model which stressed the continuities between human beings and animals. It is commonly believed that evolutionary thinking entails the view that the differences between human beings and animals are quantitative rather than qualitative. From an anatomical and physiological perspective, this is undeniably true. However, in the animal kingdom we find nothing equivalent to our cultural achievements, either in degree or kind, and this is usually attributed to the fact that we have acquired some unique characteristic—intelligence, language, symbolic activity, sentience, creativity, awareness—call it what you will. Now this difference is often blurred in our attempts to define precise and tangible traits which lie at the basis of our distinctiveness.[2] For the purposes of this argument I propose that human beings are different in at least these three respects: (1) We are not subject to the vicissitudes of natural selection to the same extent as other species; (2) We exercise freedom of choice; (3) We have a "continuity of consciousness." These last two criteria, I am aware, are neither clear nor indisputable at this point, but we shall come to them later. For the moment I wish to consider the implications of the first characteristic.

An easy case can be made that at least certain kinds and degrees of human pain exist because we are not subject to the same sorts of selection pressures as animals. Many of the pains we experience go far beyond what is necessary to ensure our survival. As well as the capacity for severe physical pain, we experience a whole range of "mental" pains—the disappointment of unrequited love, the grief of loss, the dissatisfactions and frustrations of life. These latter mental states would hardly increase an animal's chances of survival, nor indeed our own. The canons of evolutionary dogma do not enable us to entertain the view that animals might be love-sick or grief-stricken, because such behaviors would not confer any obvious selective advantage, but rather the contrary. The same is true of debilitating physical pain. Any pain or mental state which impinges upon an animal's normal routines—the things it needs to do to survive and reproduce—are counterproductive and serve no obvious function in the economy of natural selection. In human beings on the other hand, even the most severe and debilitating pains do not, in themselves, threaten our physical existence. They are part of the cost exacted for our having thwarted natural selection. It is for this reason that pain researchers have been baffled by many aspects of human pain. As a major text on pain indicates:

> ... the idea that pain is always a beneficent mechanism constitutes "an extraordinary error, which has no justification." Under conditions where it becomes nagging and persistent, pain impairs the sufferer's ability to work and to think clearly, prevents his sleep, abolishes appetite, lowers morale, and may even destroy his will to help himself survive.[3]

Pain is described by other authors as "a baleful gift" which makes the subject "more ill than he would be without it"; it is a "mystery," a "senseless element of life," and "an obstacle and a threat."[4] Pains of this type, which have no obvious survival value, we could not reasonably assume animals to experience. At the very least, then, we can say that the evolutionary model does give us grounds for asserting a significant difference between man and beast, and that our capacity to experience pain is directly related to that difference.

III

To say that animals feel less pain than we might think falls some way short of saying that they feel no pain at all. While it might be agreed that those sorts of pains which have no apparent selective justification are unique to the human species, other kinds of pains have an obvious adaptive value in that they enable us, and presumably animals, to avoid tissue damage. Those rare individuals who are born with complete insensitivity to pain experience serious injury and even death as a direct result of their condition.[5] Some pain serves a useful function. It can be reasonably assumed, *mutatis mutandis,* that pain enables animals to avoid tissue damage, and that therein lies its adaptive value. What strengthens this view is that in many instances higher animals seem to react to painful stimuli in much the same way that we do. Accordingly, we tend naturally to assume that their experience of the stimulus is similar to our own.

This common-sense analogy, however, breaks down on a number of fronts. First, we become entangled in the language of stimulus and response. Stimuli as such are not painful. Most often, painful experiences result from intense sensations from benign stimuli—heat, cold, pressure, etc.[6] "Pain," says one researcher, "may arise from virtually *any* type of stimulus or may be the result of afferent patterns which may travel via *any* available pathway."[7] More importantly, if we allow our language to be shaped by the evolutionary model, we should speak of animal responses, not as reactions to pain, or expressions of pain, but rather as adaptive behaviors and physiological reactions to potentially damaging stimuli. Their function is not primarily, or even at all, to express some internal state, but to adapt the organism behaviorally to a harmful aspect of its environment. If we adopt this admittedly cumbersome form of expression, we are in a better position to see why our common-sense analogy leads us astray— and it leads us astray in two ways. First, we tend to presume that certain animal behaviors are expressions of pain—an internal state—whereas they should properly be construed as adaptive behaviors which probably have some social significance. Second, we assume, again on the basis of our own experiences, that to produce these adaptive behaviors it is necessary for the organism to suffer pain.

The fallacy of the first assumption can be illustrated by reference to actual animal behaviors. A chimpanzee with a thorn in its foot screams out (as if in pain), while on the other hand, a wildebeest being torn apart by wild dogs or other predators dies in silence.[8] In the first instance the chimp communicates to its peers so that they might come and render aid; in the second, the opposite is the case. In each example the behavior enhances the survival of the species and it would be crudely anthropomorphic to declare that the antelope suffers with stoic dignity, while the chimpanzee screeches in a most craven fashion. On reflection, it is understood that we resist these expressions because neither the chimpanzee nor the antelope had any choice in the matter. This brings us to the second assumption— the belief that animals must suffer to produce the appropriate behaviors. If no "choice" is involved in animal behavior, why should they suffer pain— to *compel* them to behave in certain ways? No, for surely their behavior is determined in a way that does not require the superfluous promptings of pain. Again, an illustration might help us understand this principle. Every biology student learns, at one time or another, about reflex pathways.

The finger touches the hot iron. A message passes along a sensory neuron to the spinal chord where it intersects with other neurons. One impulse travels to the brain, another to an appropriate muscle. The finger is reflexively removed before any conscious action is possible. Only after or during the response is there conscious knowledge of what is taking or has taken place. The message to the brain might well be labeled "For your information." The point is that an appropriate response can be elicited without the necessity of a feeling of pain, or a conscious decision. I am not claiming with this example that all animal behavior is of this reflexive type, but rather illustrating the principle which we tend in our ways of speaking to overlook, that responses to damaging stimuli do not require the experience of pain.

What the above discussion shows is that the question we should be asking is: Why do we feel pain if animals do not? What feature of our unique status makes pain a necessary part of our existence? The answer is already provided in the determined nature of animal behavior. What is distinctive about the human race is our ability to choose, to determine our priorities, to be above unreflective reaction. We are free, in painful situations, to damage our bodies if we believe that there is a higher priority. We have the choice because in human life there are considerations more important than our survival, and these considerations arise out of our not being subject to selection pressures as are animals. Pain frees us from the compulsion of acting instinctively; it issues harsh warnings, but they are warnings which may be ignored. It is our capacity for pain which has given rise to those uniquely human attributes of courage, resignation, self-control, perseverance, endurance, and their opposites, and it is significant that we reserve these terms for ourselves. . . .

IV

With the failure of the analogical case for animal pain, there remains one argument to be answered before we progress to the outright assertion that animals do not suffer pain. While there are important differences between man and beast, the extent to which the differences are reflected anatomically and physiologically is minimal. It has been argued that the functioning of the nervous systems of the higher animals so closely resembles our own that there can be little doubt that these creatures feel pain as we do.[9] This case is strengthened by the fact that pain research carried out on animals can be applied to human beings. Moreover, our pain killers are tested on animals and animals can be conditioned by "pain." . . .

From earliest times there has been discussion of whether pain can properly be categorized as a sensation. Aristotle thought not, and discussed it in the context of virtue. Spinoza deemed it an emotion. In our own century, Ryle has similarly argued that we are mistaken when we categorize pain with sensations.[10] It has long been recognized, in other words, that pain is associated with "higher" faculties, the study of which is more properly psychological than physiological. The importance of this association has been brought home by a number of studies on the psychology of pain.

The pain of childbirth, for example, commonly held to be one of the most severe kinds of pain, is almost negligible for women in some cultures. In certain instances the man experiences pain and remains in bed with the baby while the woman returns to her normal duties.[11] There are, moreover, considerable differences in "pain thresholds" for different individuals, which are related to a variety of non-physiological variables.[12] Similarly, individuals in ecstatic or hypnotic states, sportsmen and soldiers at the peak of the game or the battle often simply do not "feel" pain as they might under more normal circumstances.[13] The operation of certain analgesic drugs is also suggestive. Opiate painkillers act not upon nerve impulses carrying messages of "pain" to the brain, but upon the "psychological context" of the pain. Placebos seem to work in much the same way.[14] I cite this evidence not in order to argue that animals are like human beings in ecstatic or drugged states, but rather to show that our feelings of pain are not simply a function of neuroanatomy, but also of psychological and cultural factors—factors which could play but a minimal role in animals' lives. There is no simple equation from equivalent physiology to equivalent experience of pain. More than this, however, these examples show that at least in some cases it is our human consciousness which determines whether certain nerve impulses will cause suffering or not. Nor is it a question of mind over matter, as if our consciousness can somehow override the "natural" experience of pain. This is redolent of Cartesian dualism. In fact, ironically, it is partly the residual influence of Cartesian thinking which leads us to persist in attributing the experience of pain to animals. We sunder physical pain from other aspects of human suffering, assuming that it belongs to our bodies while other sorts of pains—bereavement, anxiety, frustration—belong to our minds. Because animals have bodies but no minds, or so we think, we assume that they share our bodily pains but not our mental pains. All human experiences of pain,

I have argued, are functions of our distinctive consciousness, and thus cannot be shared by our furry friends.

I am not alone in espousing this particular view of human suffering. David Bakan, for example, observes that:

> . . . unless there is a psyche, unless there is an awake and conscious organism, there is nothing to which one can sensibly refer as pain. Pain exists only in a conscious ego. . . .
>
> Pain, having no other locus but the conscious ego, is almost literally the price man pays for the possession of a conscious ego. . . .[15]

Wittgenstein expresses a similar sentiment in this way:

> Pain has *this* position in our life; has *these* connections; (That is to say: we only call "pain" what has *this* position, *these* connections).
>
> Only surrounded by certain normal manifestations of life, is there such a thing as an expression of pain. Only surrounded by an even more far-reaching particular manifestation of life, such a thing as the expression of sorrow or affection. And so on.[16]

What I have tried to do is to point out the implications of such views for the problem of animal pain.

V

By now it should be clear that there are good reasons for questioning the traditional view that animals feel pain. The difficulty is that our language and many of our practices conspire to maintain us in that traditional belief. We are unable to envisage what it must be like for a patient not to feel pain, and yet react as if it does. In this last section I want to see if we can conceptualize what it might mean to encounter a painful stimulus, to react to it (physiologically and behaviorally), and yet not feel pain. This is, admittedly, a speculative exercise, but I believe that our own experiences can show that this state of affairs is possible, and even probable in the case of animals. Consider the following three examples.

Jones has the most terrible nightmares. It is common for him to cry out in fear, to moan as if in pain, even to break into a cold sweat as he sleeps. He never wakes during these episodes, and upon waking in the morning has no recollection of them. (Psychologists inform us that we only remember dreams if we wake up during or shortly after them.) Jones only knows of his nocturnal behavior because he is informed of it by his observant and long-suffering wife. On being told that he has had another of his frightful nightmares his only reaction is one of mild curiosity, and concern that his wife has lost sleep. There is no sense in which he feels that he has "suffered" during the night, that he has felt fear or pain, for there is no conscious continuity between his waking self and his dreaming self. Whatever the external signs might lead us to think about his mental state, there is no "experience" of this mental state which the waking Jones regards as being of any significance. Now, you might say, this is because the "pain" and "fear" in Jones's dream were illusory. In a sense this is true, and Jones would agree, but without access to Jones's own thoughts on the matter we would probably infer from his reactions that he was undergoing an unpleasant experience, albeit "in his mind." This might prompt us to ask if there were any circumstances under which Jones might experience those nightmares as pain, for otherwise it might be objected that our example was not really analogous to pain, but rather dreams about pain. We are asking, in other words, if dreams about pain (nightmares) can really be painful. I think we can elaborate our example to show that they can. One night, Jones wakes in the middle of one of his nightmares, and for the first time is conscious of his own reactions. He feels his heart pounding, the sweat on his brow, he personally identifies with the victim of his dream. Having woken in mid-dream, Jones has established a link between his "waking self" and his "sleeping self," and he can now "own" the terror which "he" experienced in his dream. In that no-man's-land between waking state and dreaming, Jones has been able to correlate the physical reactions which his wife habitually observed, with his own inner state—that is, the Jones of everyday, waking existence. What is the difference then, between experiencing a bad nightmare and merely showing signs of experiencing a bad nightmare? The answer has to do with continuity of consciousness. Animal "awareness" thus might be something like a succession of dream states.

A second example concerns a hypothetical drug which we shall call an "amnesiesthetic." This is a drug which works on both the voluntary nervous system, to induce paralysis, and the memory, to bring about memory loss.[17] Let us suppose that doctors come to rely on amnesiesthetics to replace conventional anesthetics in surgery because their side-effects are virtually nil. The operation of amnesiesthetics, we should bear in mind, is quite different from that of conventional anesthetics. The new drug seems merely to paralyze the patient during surgery, and then wipe out all of his memories of the event. Whether the patient experiences any pain during the operation seems to be a moot point, for while there is no way for the patient to communicate his experiences during the course of the operation, upon recovery there is no recollection of what took place on the operating table. The anti-vivisectionists might take up cudgels against the new practice, but it would be unlikely that they could find patients to testify against the use of the drug, for none recall having experienced any pain and most are grateful that they were free of the side-effects of more conventional anesthetics. To all intents and purposes, amnesiesthetics give the same results as anesthetics without the side effects. For the patient to "own" the pain of surgery, again, some continuity must exist between the patient who is undergoing surgery, and the patient who is recovering from surgery. The drug acts to break this continuity of identity, and thus while a patient might grant that *pain was experienced* during the operation, he would not be inclined to say: *I experienced pain.* I do not mean to imply here that animals suffer chronic forgetfulness and cannot recall their pain, for this would imply that they would also fail to recall things that they had learned. Rather they are like (hypothetical) chronic amnesiacs, who lose their identity at every instant of time. A chronic amnesiac, we might suppose, could not own the pain of a previous self, yet could still walk, talk, drive a car and do many of the things that he or she had learned as a previous self. There is continuity of a kind in higher animals, for how else could they learn, but this does not entail owning the pain of the lessons learned.

One final example concerns personal identity and early childhood. There are things from my childhood which I can recall, there are some which I could in principle recall, but which I have forgotten, and there are some events which I cannot recall, and could not possibly recall. My inability to recollect events in my fetal life, or in my earliest childhood, is not due to defects in my memory, but rather results from the fact that there was no single identity to which all my various "experiences" could belong. I assume, as a baby, that I had many painful experiences. Birth presumably caused me some discomfort, as did that battery of injections which I received soon after. But like Jones, who slept blissfully through his nasty nightmares, or the amnesiesthetized patient who knows nothing of the pain of surgery, I cannot "own" those painful experiences. I am not implying here that painful experiences which are forgotten were never painful to start with. The pain of that very first injection is of quite a different status from that injection which I received when I was four, but have since forgotten. When I was four I had the ability to correlate a whole range of sensations and conceive of them as happening to *me*. There was, at that later time, not simply a painful stimulus and an appropriate response, but an ongoing context in which that event took place, and a conscious "I" who was the recipient of the stimulus, and the initiator of the response. The continuity of my present self does not extend back to birth or beyond, but to some time after; hence I am unable to own those early experiences of pain, unable to say "they *happened to me.*"

Irrespective of the way we speak about babies and pain, a number of our practices show that we regard neonatal pain as less significant than pain which is experienced later in life. Birth, it is agreed, is a time of great pain for the mother, but little sympathy is directed towards the child. If you are told that yours was a painful birth, it is not because you are perceived to be the recipient of pain, rather, if anything, the cause of it. So too, conventional wisdom dictates that the early years are the best time for circumcision, and few circumcised males would disagree. At a different level, if your father dies when you are one year old, no one in later years will offer condolences on account of the grief you must have suffered. (You may well have suffered as a result of not having a father, but you would not as a one-year-old have suffered *bereavement.*) We tend to say of this example "Ah, but you were too young to know what was really happening." Surely this sentiment is as true of physical pain as of mental pain.

This last example is crucial, because it is during our earliest stages of development that our awareness is most like that of the higher animals. At least the evolutionary maxim "ontogeny recapitulates phylogeny" (the development of organisms mirrors their evolutionary history) gives some justification for asserting this. Our own early experiences, or lack thereof, thus provide a link between these otherwise hypothetical states of consciousness and animal life.

The force of these examples should by now be apparent. The "awareness" of animals is like that of the sleeping Jones, the amnesiesthetized patient, the neonate. They encounter painful stimuli, they react to them, but there is nothing to which that pain can belong. The animal, and, dare I say it, the neonate, have no self, and their pains are rather successive states which lack the connection which would render them "painful experiences."[18] Putting it more formally:

1. Continuity of experience is the crucial aspect of the human awareness of pain.
2. Animals lack that continuity of experience, and therefore,
3. Animals do not experience pain as we do.

. . . If animals lack a continuity of identity as I have suggested, we might wonder how it is that they can learn from painful experiences, for we tend naturally to think that there must be something to recall the pain of a past event and correlate it with a present one. Again, I believe this natural way of thinking to be mistaken, for it involves a faulty concept of memory. Our "chronic amnesiacs," for example, recall past lessons but not past identities/pains. In any case, we need only consider the learning processes of some organisms to see that this assumption is wrong. The very simplest of organisms—the *Protozoa*—exhibit rudimentary learning in their ability to distinguish habitual stimuli from novel stimuli. Once these habitual stimuli are identified, the organisms no longer react to them.[19] Thus, habituation, admittedly the simplest kind of learning, is displayed by single-celled organisms in which there is not even a nervous system, far less what we might call "awareness" or "memory." I am not claiming here that all learning processes work in the same way as those of the *Protozoa*, but simply making the general point that learning can take place without the requirement of consciousness. . . .

The view of animal pain which I have outlined here has a number of implications. It should not be thought that I am advocating that we beat our infants and pets. There are other moral considerations which show this kind of behavior to be wrong irrespective of what patients feel. On the other hand, if my view of animal pain is correct, such causes as animal liberation may need to be rethought. . . .

NOTES

1. René Descartes, *A Discourse on Method*, trans. John Veitch (London: Dent, 1957) pt. v (44ff.); Letter CXCII (to Mersenne), in *Oeuvres de Descartes*, ed. Charles Adam and Paul Tannery (Paris: L. Cerf, 1897–1913) III, p. 85.
2. We ask the question: What is it by virtue of which we differ from the animals? The answer is given: Intelligence. But what is "Intelligence"? Intelligence is defined. But animal X displays intelligence. Oh, perhaps it is the ability to use language, then. But Lucy the chimpanzee was able to learn American Sign Language. Could the difference be Creativity . . . ? And so the original distinction

is forgotten in our concern to label an attribute which accounts for our being different.

3. J. C. White and W. H. Sweet, *Pain: Its Mechanisms and Neurosurgical Control* (Springfield, Ill.: Charles C. Thomas, 1955), p. 68.

4. Reńe Leriche, *The Surgery of Pain,* ed. and trans. by Archibald Young (Baltimore: Williams and Wilkins, 1939), p. 23; F. J. J. Buytendijk, *Pain: Its Modes and Functions* (University of Chicago Press, 1962), p. 40.

5. On chronic insensitivity to pain and its consequences, see Ronald Melzak, *The Puzzle of Pain* (New York: Basic Books, 1973), pp. 15–16.

6. See ibid., p. 85.

7. W. Noordenbos, *Pain: Problems Pertaining to the Transmission of Nerve Impulses Which Give Rise to Pain* (New York: Elsevier Publishing Co., 1959), p. 176.

8. David McFarland, "Pain," *The Oxford Companion to Animal Behavior,* ed. David MacFarland (Oxford University Press, 1981), p. 439.

9. See, e.g., John Hick, *Evil and the God of Love* (London: Fontana, 1968), pp. 346f.; Richard Serjeant, *The Spectrum of Pain* (London: Hart-Davis, 1969), p. 72; Peter Singer, *Animal Liberation* (London: Jonathan Cape, 1976), pp. 13f.

10. Aristotle, *Nicomachean Ethics,* Bk. II, ch. iii; Bk. III, ch. xi; Baruch de Spinoza, *Ethics* III, prop. 1v; Gilbert Ryle, *The Concept of Mind* (New York: Barnes and Noble, 1949), p. 203.

11. Melzak, *The Puzzle of Pain,* p. 22. Cf. Grantly Dick-Read, *Childbirth Without Fear* (New York: Dell, 1962).

12. J. W. Clark and D. Bindra, "Individual Differences in Pain Thresholds," *Canadian Journal of Psychology* 10 (1956): pp. 69–81.

13. Melzak, *The Puzzle of Pain,* pp. 29–31.

14. Harris Hill et al., "Studies on Anxiety Associated with Anticipation of Pain: Effects of Morphine," *AMA Archives of Neurology and Psychiatry* 67 (1952): 612–19; Cf. Henry K. Beecher, *Measurement of Subjective Responses: Quantitative Effects of Drugs* (New York: Oxford University Press, 1959), passim.

15. David Bakan, *Disease, Pain and Sacrifice: Toward a Psychology of Suffering* (University of Chicago Press, 1968), p. 70.

16. Ludwig Wittgenstein, *Zettel* (Berkeley: University of California Press, 1970), Nos. 533, 534 (94ff.). Cf. Ivan Illich: "The act of suffering pain always has a [sic] historical dimension," *Limits to Medicine* (Ringwood: Penguin, 1977), p. 148.

17. Wittgenstein once asked what difference it would make if anesthetics only made us forget pain. This example is developed from that question.

18. If I read him correctly, this is a line of argument which C. S. Lewis also adopts. See his *The Problem of Pain* (London: Fontana, 1957), pp. 119f.

19. Nicholas Mackintosh, "Learning," *Oxford Companion to Animal Behavior,* p. 337.

Part Four

Positions and Proposals

13

Animal Research:
A Position Statement

Richard H. Schwarz

The following position statement was recently adopted by the deans of 13 medical schools that make up the Associated Medical Schools of New York. The statement was drawn up in response to concerns expressed by faculty members over the continuing pressure from extremist groups in the animal rights movement, which has disrupted research in a number of institutions.

The Deans of the Associated Medical Schools of New York reaffirm in the strongest terms the obligation of our institutions to carry on the research programs that have expanded our knowledge of disease and led to life saving therapies. The use of laboratory animals is indispensable to much of this work, and we are gravely concerned that the actions of some organizations espousing an "animal rights" philosophy will threaten the continued progress of biomedical research.

In recent months, we have seen pressure from such extremist organizations disrupt ongoing research projects supported by public funds. Leadership among medical schools and universities must stand firm in

From *Science*, Letter to the Editor, 244 (June 9, 1989): 1128. Copyright © 1989 by The American Association for the Advancement of Science. Reprinted by permission.

the face of this pressure and insist that our institutions fully live up to the obligations they incur when they accept public and private research support.

AMS fully acknowledges that, along with the responsibility to fulfill our research role is the need for stewardship on behalf of those animals which are so vital to this work. All institutions conducting research must enforce appropriate standards for the care and use of laboratory animals. Research centers are currently subject to extensive laws, policies, guidelines and accreditation standards dealing with the use of animals in research.

The documentation of the benefits of such research not only to humankind, but also to animals themselves, is unchallengeable. Our disagreement is not with advocates of appropriate and respectful use of animals in a manner consistent with established guidelines for animal welfare, but with extremists who insist that no circumstances exist under which we can morally differentiate between the worth of the life of a human being and that of an animal. Such a philosophy is out of harmony with the tenets of most religions and codes of behavior in the world, and with the majority view in our society. Moreover, we cannot tolerate tactics of intimidation and violence which undermine our democratic traditions and threaten the principle of free scientific inquiry.

AMS pledges to the faculty in our member institutions that we will use every resource in our command to protect and preserve the right of scientists to pursue knowledge for the good of all people. Animal rights activists, no matter how well intentioned, will not be permitted to subvert the established mechanisms for conduct of responsible animal research and erode our obligations to society as physicians and scientists.

R. H. S.
President,
Associated Medical Schools of New York,
70 West 36th Street, Suite 302
New York, NY 10018

14

To Do or Not to Do?

Peter Singer

In 1939 Otto Schmidt was working as a laboratory assistant at a distinguished medical research institute in Germany. He learned, through chance remarks and his own observation, that another unit of the institute was receiving mentally retarded persons from a nearby asylum, and using them as research subjects. The patients were exposed to various poisonous gases, including nerve gas, and then forced to continue walking up and down an inclined ramp. They frequently vomited, and showed other symptoms of illness; but if they stopped, they were beaten with sticks. After a few days, most patients died from the poison gases they had inhaled; the remainder were put to death.

Schmidt was horrified by his discovery. At first he assumed that the scientists carrying out this research were doing so without authority, and that if the authorities were informed, it would be stopped. But his initial attempts to act on this assumption failed when the director of the institute made it clear that he had special permission from the highest levels to carry out this research "in the interests of the German soldier, who may again be exposed to chemical warfare." Schmidt attempted to contact these higher authorities, but he received no response. He also tried to alert

From *Hastings Center Report* (November/December 1989):42–44. Copyright © 1989 The Hastings Center. Reprinted by permission of the publisher and the author.

the relatives of the patients, but his inquiries revealed that only patients who had no contact with relatives were selected for the experiments.

There was little more, legally, that Schmidt could do, but the experiments were continuing, and he could not simply forget about them. Therefore he decided on the only course of action he could think of that stood a chance of stopping the experiments. The unit conducting the experiments was housed in a separate, and specially equipped, building. One night, when neither staff nor experimental subjects were in the building, Otto obtained a supply of petrol and set fire to the building. His plan was entirely successful; the building was destroyed, and because of shortages of resources at the time, never rebuilt. No further experiments with poison gases were conducted at that research institute.

What attitude should we take to what Otto Schmidt did? In criticism of his actions, it might be argued that he broke the law of his own country. Although he had certainly attempted to use legal channels to stop the research, it could not be said that he had exhausted all legal channels, since he had not received a definite and final response to his letters to higher authorities. It may also be said that Schmidt caused the destruction of a costly scientific research facility, and stopped a scientific research project that was adding to our knowledge about the capacities of human beings to continue working after exposure to harmful chemicals. Schmidt was not qualified, it might plausibly be asserted, to assess the scientific value of this work, nor its importance to the German Army.

Yet I do not think many of us will find these criticisms convincing. Schmidt was witnessing an atrocity. While the subjects of the experiments were suffering every day, he could not be expected to wait indefinitely for an official response—especially since this response might well be that the project should continue. As for the claim that Schmidt was not qualified to judge the value of the project, in this particular situation it seems clear that the project was unjustifiable. Schmidt did indeed use his own moral judgment on this matter, but his judgment was sound. For this—and also, of course, for his personal courage—he deserves not criticism, but the highest praise.

Now consider a more recent incident:

At a prestigious research institute in the United States, monkeys were trained to run in a cylindrical treadmill. The monkeys received electric shocks unless they kept the treadmill moving. Once the monkeys had completed initial training at keeping the treadmill in motion, they were subjected to varying doses of radiation. Monkeys receiving the higher doses vomited repeatedly. They were then put back into the treadmill to measure the effect of the radiation on their ability to keep it moving. During this period, if a monkey did not move the treadmill for one minute, shock intensity was increased to 10 mA. (This is an intense electric shock, causing severe pain.) Some monkeys continued to vomit while in the treadmill. The irradiated monkeys took up to five days to die.

Animal liberationists learned that the institute was conducting these experiments. For several years they protested against them through a variety of legal channels, without success. Then an animal activist—let us call her Olivia Smith—succeeded in entering the laboratory in which these experiments were carried out and caused such damage to the laboratory and its equipment that the experiments stopped and were not resumed.

What attitude should we take to what Olivia Smith did? If we think that Schmidt was a hero, should we also think of Smith in the same way?

The criticisms noted in relation to Otto Schmidt's action will also be pressed against Olivia Smith. Do they have greater validity in her case than in his? Those who want to argue that Schmidt was a hero, but at the same time want to condemn Smith, will probably appeal first to the fact that the victims for whom Schmidt acted were human beings, whereas those saved by Smith's act were monkeys. I have elsewhere argued—and many other philosophers now agree—that species *in itself* cannot be a basis for this kind of distinction. It may be legitimate to treat differently beings with different capacities; but the mere fact that one being is a member of our species, and another being is not, cannot justify us in inflicting pain and death on the latter in circumstances that would not justify us in inflicting pain and death on the former.[1]

So can we appeal to differences in the capacities of the beings involved in the experiments that took place in Germany and in the United States? We could only do this if our judgment about Schmidt's action was based on knowledge about the capacities of the subjects of the experiments he stopped. But we have no information on this matter—the subjects were described as mentally retarded, but how severely was not stated. Obviously, they were capable of walking, and of feeling pain. Equally obviously, so were the monkeys in the American experiment. There is no basis on which we can be confident that the human subjects were superior in respect of rationality, awareness, or any other possibly relevant capacity, to the nonhumans. In any case, if we were able to decide that Schmidt's actions were justified without inquiring more closely into the mental capacities of the human subjects, this strongly suggests that the existence of higher mental capacities—beyond the capacity to feel pain and to suffer from the poisonous gases—was not really relevant to our judgment. Accordingly, I conclude that our knowledge of any differences between the experimental subjects, whether in species or in capacities, is insufficient to serve as a basis for sharply differing judgments about what Schmidt and Smith did.

The other factor likely to be put forward in explanation of why Schmidt was fully justified but Smith was not, is that Germany in 1939 was not a democracy, and there was no proper channel for stopping the experiments; in the United States, on the other hand, there are adequate opportunities for bringing about change through the democratic process. The differences between the political systems are of immense significance. Although the United States is far from being a perfect democracy, we rightly treasure the opportunities it offers for peacefully and legitimately changing the laws of the country. In a society like the United States the obligation to try to bring about change by democratic means is very strong. If Olivia Smith's action had not been preceded by a long period of attempting to stop such experiments by lawful means, it would have been wrong. But such efforts *had* been made. They had been unavailing. The monkeys were continuing to go through extreme pain and suffering in the course of an experiment that was highly unlikely to bring significant benefits to humans or animals. In such circumstances, is the obligation to use only democratic means to bring about change an absolute one?

Though I am a strong supporter of democratic systems of government, even imperfect ones, I cannot believe that the obligation to use only democratic means is absolute. During the period of the civil rights marches, and later of protest against the Vietnam war, millions of Americans supported illegal forms of protest. Many of these involved breaches of racist segregation laws, and of the draft laws; some also caused damage to property, both private and government. It may be questioned whether such tactics were the most effective means possible to achieve civil rights for blacks, or to end the war in Vietnam; but this is a matter of strategy, not of ethics. If we can assume, for the sake of argument, that they were the *only* possible means of achieving those goals in a reasonable period of time, were they justified? I think they were. Even in a democracy, we can be justified in taking unlawful means to bring about change.

There is, I believe, a line to be drawn between acts that are illegal (including acts that cause specific and limited damage to property), and acts that inflict physical violence on others. A sound democracy can tolerate a certain amount of illegal protest; but violence against others is always likely to escalate quickly. More important still, when those who are acting on an ethical basis resort to violence, they obscure the clarity of their ethical stand and send a confused message to the public. Under a repressive dictatorship there may be no alternative to violence; but in a democracy, to resort to violence is to put in peril values that are greater than almost any cause.

Since Olivia Smith avoided inflicting physical violence on anyone, her act was not on the wrong side of this line. There may have been a much heavier burden of justification on Olivia Smith than on Otto Schmidt, but if her act, like his, was the only way to end an atrocity, she may also have been justified in what she did.

This is not a view I reach lightly.To encourage people to take the law into their own hands is a dangerous thing. There will be many people who regard as an atrocity acts that I do not see in the same light. Abortion is one obvious example. People who believe that a prenatal human being has the same right to life as an older human being are, in my view, misguided.[2] In that respect I see a greater difference between Otto Schmidt and a pro-life activist who burns down an abortion clinic than I do between Otto Schmidt and Olivia Smith. Yet it is impossible to convince many pro-life people that they are mistaken, and so from their perspective, they too are entitled to the praise we bestow upon Otto Schmidt.

Reflecting on the position of those who do not share our views about what is right and what is wrong is salutary, because it makes us realize how great a responsibility we are under to think and think again about the judgment that what is happening is not merely wrong, but *so* wrong that it justifies taking the law into one's own hands. But where that judgment is clear; where it is a judgment that other reasonable people, fully informed of the facts of the situation, will share; where there is no other way of halting a continuing atrocity; where care is taken to avoid physical violence against anyone; then, and only then, do I believe direct action to be justifiable.

Otto Schmidt and Olivia Smith are imaginary, as are the German experiments I described. But I did not invent the experiments on monkeys. My account is drawn from a paper entitled "Effects of Mixed Neutron-gamma Total-body Irradiation on Physical Activity Performance of Rhesus Monkeys," published in *Radiation Research* in 1985.[3] The experiments took place at the Armed Forces Radiobiology Institute, in Bethesda, Maryland. As far as I am aware, similar experiments are still continuing.

NOTES

1. See *Animal Liberation* (New York: New York Review/Random House, 1975, revised edition, 1989), chap. 1; or *Practical Ethics* (Cambridge: Cambridge University Press, 1979), chap. 3.

2. See *Practical Ethics*, chap. 6.

3. Vol. 101, pp. 434–41.

15

Some Ethical Concerns in Animal Research: Where Do We Go Next?

Bernard E. Rollin

While it is very tempting to debate the extremes over whether animals should or should not be used for research, the real progress, as occurs in all social issues, will take place by way of incremental changes instituted in response to increasing public sophistication concerning the diverse and subtle ethical issues involved in animal experimentation. My remarks today will be aimed at highlighting a number of areas that must be clarified prior to rational implementation of viable changes, as well as at suggesting plausible pathways along which progress can occur.

In the first place, all parties to the discussion must become aware that, at root, however emotional the issues may be, they can and must be dealt with rationally, as can all issues of social morality. Such a realization is difficult for all parties concerned, but perhaps most difficult for the research community, primarily for historical reasons. Like all other human activities, science rests upon certain assumptions that are taken for granted by its practitioners, who are usually too busy making progress using the assumptions to take much time to examine them. (Such examination falls to those strange ducks known as philosophers.) And one major

---

This paper was delivered at San Francisco State University, May 1990.

assumption that has dominated twentieth-century science, which I have examined in detail elsewhere, is the claim that science is value-free, that scientists *qua* scientists do not deal with value judgments, since such judgments are not testable and are simply matters of unverifiable "opinion." Scientists know that science deals with hard data, with *facts*—this is what demarcates it from theology, metaphysics, and all forms of unfounded speculation and, as Wittgenstein once remarked, one can collect all the facts in the universe and not find the fact that "killing is wrong." As a result, scientists have tended to eschew discussion of ethical issues, leaving such discussions and judgments, as scientists working on the Manhattan Project remarked, to the politicians.

Even the most cursory examination of scientific writings of all sorts patently buttresses my claim that scientists qua scientists distance themselves from ethics. Keeton and Gould, for example, in their widely used freshmen biology text, remark that "science cannot make value judgments . . . and cannot make moral judgments."[1] In the same vein, Mader, in her basic biology text, asserts that "science does not make ethical or moral decisions."[2] Last year, James Wyngarden, former director of NIH [National Institutes of Health], declared that all the flap about genetic engineering was misdirected, for "science should not be hampered by ethical judgments."[3] In 1988, Richard Marocco, a psychological researcher at the University of Oregon, responded to critics of animal research by asserting that their concern was "not an intellectual concern—it's an emotional, an ethical one, and a moral one,"[4] as if ethical concerns were not suited for rational adjudication.

Given this ideology, it is not surprising that the research community is often uncomfortable and inarticulate in its discussion of burgeoning social ethical concerns. As Dr. Jay Katz at Yale has documented, the medical research community failed to see the moral issues in the use of human subjects for research until forced to address them by threat of legislation.[5] And few scientific journals, conferences, or courses proactively discuss the ethical questions engendered by their activity. (I was astounded to learn from the Office of Technology Assessment of Congress that my 1985 paper on the ethical issues raised in the genetic engineering of animals was the only paper on the subject published in the United States.)[6] Nor is it surprising that leading scientists often say silly things about moral questions—hence, Dr. Donald Kennedy's incredible non sequitur about critics of animal research, namely, that "antivivisection was one of the policies of the Hitler regime."[7] (As one of my students remarked, Hitler also had a mustache.)

Plainly the use of animals in biomedical research does involve moral value judgments on the part of those researchers who use animals. As an obvious example, every animal researcher who employs an animal in an invasive or terminal protocol must make the implicit moral judgment that the knowledge or benefit gained from the research is more important than or outweighs the suffering or death exacted from the animals. And if, as researchers often argue, biomedical science is at least at present conceptually inseparable from the invasive use of animals, then there is a moral judgment at the very basis of biomedicine, and one can hardly maintain the position that such science is value-free.

Since society as a whole has begun to realize that invasive animal use by humans raises moral issues, science has been forced to acknowledge such questions at least nominally. Indeed, stimulating such acknowledgment was a major thrust behind the 1985 federal laboratory animal legislation I and my colleagues helped to draft. And some progress has been made. No longer do researchers matter-of-factly proclaim, as some scientists did fairly recently, that research animals are simply tools whose feelings don't matter. But such an admission is only an acknowledgment of the problem—daily discussion and pondering of the multiplicity of ethical questions raised by its activities must be built into scientific education, practice, and publication.

At least some spokespersons for the research community have made a rational attempt to address the issues growing out of invasive animal use. Typical of these responses was one by Dr. Theodore Cooper[8] of the Association for Biomedical Research in his response to a paper by Dr. Andrew Rowan and myself.[9]

Dr. Cooper's response in essence rests upon two components: first, that society values human life over animal life; and second, that the cost to animals used in research is outweighed by the benefit that accrues to humans and other animals. In other words, Dr. Cooper makes explicit the ethical judgment that we earlier indicated was presuppositional to animal research. And this brings me to the second major point I want to make. . . . It is probably true that society in general does value human life over animal life. And it is also doubtless true that great benefit sometimes emerges from animal research. But does this therefore provide adequate justification for such research, given the tissue of ethical beliefs we in society hold? If it did, society would have similar justification for doing involuntary invasive research on humans who are valued less than mainstream humans. All societies do have such a hierarchy of value. Nazi

Germany, for example, valued Jews, Slavs, gypsies, and retarded people far lower than Aryans. Let us further suppose, as was indeed sometimes the case, that such Nazi research produced great benefits. Would we then ipso facto view such work as justified? Clearly not—witness the recent unwillingness of the EPA [Environmental Protection Agency] to use Nazi data for our benefit. Please note that I am not comparing animal researchers to Nazis; I am simply arguing that, in our society's ethic, being viewed as less valuable than others does not mean that your interests can be sacrificed to the more valuable—we would not seize a derelict's heart even to save Mother Theresa. In other words, in our ethical machinery, which is being extended in society to apply to our treatment of animals, being worth less does not mean you can be sacrificed to those who are worth more or even to the general welfare, if you are a moral object at all, and strict utilitarian calculation of benefits emerging from such exploitation does not suffice to justify it. Hence our society's ethic would not allow torture of the most despicable terrorist who had planted a bomb in an elementary school, even to extract information regarding the location of the device, even if hundreds of innocent children would suffer if we fail to find it.

In other words, given the logic of our social ethic, with its emphasis on protecting all individual objects of moral concern, even the most disvalued are protected from having their basic interests sacrificed to the general welfare. And given our recent social tendency to apply the ethic to animals, Cooper's argument must be suspect. General welfare does not obviously trump moral concern for the most basic aspects of the lives of those falling within the sphere of applicability of our moral ideas.

Nonetheless, Cooper might argue, as researchers do, that the extent of application of our moral machinery to animals is still at issue, and at the moment one can therefore argue that the cost-benefit argument does justify animal research. This brings me to my third point, a very practical recommendation for the next stage of public policy. If, indeed, the best argument that can be offered at the moment on behalf of invasive animal research is the claim for patent outweighing of costs by benefits, it should be a matter of policy that only invasive research that clearly meets those conditions should be permitted. In other words, the next natural step in the evolution of the dialectic on animal research is to assure that only patently beneficial animal research would be permitted.

Obviously, this criterion would exclude a great deal of current invasive animal research, ranging from much, if not most, product testing to military research, to a great deal of "knowledge-for-its-own-sake" research. But this seems to me to be a logical conclusion, not only of the new social concern for animals, but also of the *researchers' own defense for animal research.*

The researcher who does not like this conclusion will probably invoke an obvious response here: "Your point is well taken if we indeed knew which research was likely to result in what benefits. The trouble is, we can't make such predictions. There are numerous examples of totally unexpected benefits serendipitously arising out of projects in ways no one could possibly have anticipated." While this is historically true, it is not an adequate response. For if that argument were cogent, we could not ever decide what research to fund and not to fund, even independently of the morality of animal use! The point is, we have limited resources. When we fund research into the molecular biology of the AIDS virus, but not into the health effects of wearing four-leaf clovers, we make a decision based on probabilities and plausibilities, not on serendipity. The majority of research proposals are not funded, precisely because we judge that A and B will be less valuable than C. The same sorts of calculations could and should be exported to the area of animal research. While I personally believe that *any* sort of cost-benefit reckoning is fraught with conceptual difficulty, I see no intrinsic additional difficulty in judging animal research by the criteria mentioned above. Obviously, certain new ethical questions would need to be dealt with more seriously than they have been addressed in the past. For example, in calculating cost benefit of animal research, how would one weigh painless death of animals that involved no suffering? (This is unclear even to philosophers who debate this issue.) How does one weigh the benefit of understanding some very basic biological process that might eventually result in new therapeutic or preventive medical strategies? These are difficult questions, but one thing is certain—demanding such cost-benefit justification for research on animals would surely spur the development of noninvasive alternatives by those pursuing questions where the benefits are not obvious.

The demand for such cost-benefit policy as we have sketched gives rise to my fourth major point—who is to assess such cost-benefit claims? Currently, of course, competing claims for funding are adjudicated by panels of experts in the given field. It is well known that such procedures tend toward conservatism, toward favoring the status quo, toward preserving established paradigms and approaches, and toward in-group domination of a field. Such an approach therefore is unlikely to implement the new sort of calculation we have argued for. I would therefore argue that funding decisions should be made not by experts, but by the citizenry that pays for research. I would defend the development of panels—grand juries as it were—of intelligent, interested citizens who would look at research proposals and decide if the benefits exceeded the costs, or if the question being asked was the sort that truly needed to be answered. Obviously, such panels would need expert advice to assure that the project was technically feasible, and to translate what was being proposed into nontechnical notions. But, having gotten such information, they would be asked to judge the project in accordance with emerging concern for animals and the cost-benefit notions outlined above. Such a mechanism would do much to move science away from elitism and old boyism and closer to its democratic funding base. It would also assure the ingression of changing ethical ideas into the fabric of science and hasten the erosion of the idea that science was "value-free."

Most researchers are aghast at such a proposal, for they are used to justifying what they do only to experts. Yet in my view, such a system would be salubrious. Not only would it benefit animals, but it would also integrate science and concern for science far more closely into the fabric of society and help accelerate scientific literacy.

To recapitulate: we have thus far argued that there is a need for greater attention into ethical questions in animal research on the part of scientists. Such ethical attention inevitably leads to the question of justification of invasive animal research. The form generally taken in such justification by scientists is to cite major benefits of animal research. It therefore follows that the next logical step in regulation of animal research is to set up a mechanism to assure that only invasive research that is likely to engender patently more benefit than cost be permitted, though even this should continue to occasion ethical unease given that our ethic does not permit encroachment on a few humans for the sake of the many. We have further argued that such cost-benefit decisions should be made by democratic representatives of the public, not by experts.

The fifth point I wish to make focuses on a trend already identifiable in recent (1985) federal laboratory animal legislation.[10] It has been pointed out by people like Dr. Tom Wolfle at NIH that, contrary to widespread belief, not all animal research is invasive, and that animals often suffer far more from being kept under conditions inimical to their natures than from research manipulation.[11] This suggests that the research community must continue to pursue vigorously the federal mandate toward keeping animals happy and comfortable in research facilities, instantiated in the requirement that dogs receive exercise and primates be housed under conditions that enhance their psychological well-being. This point is one that I have stressed since the mid-1970s—if we are going to use animals for research or indeed for agriculture or in zoos, we are obliged to do the utmost possible towards respecting the fundamental interests constitutive of their *telos* or nature. . . . And so laboratory animals must be protected not only against overt pain and suffering, but also against boredom and social deprivation as well, and given the opportunity to express their natures. Here the interests of the animals coincide with the interests of scientists; the more congenial the environment is to an animal, the more one has minimized variables that can confound one's results' . . . .

My final point concerns another area of husbandry of laboratory animals that hasn't been sufficiently addressed either by the research community or by animal advocates. I am referring here to the new technical capability emerging from genetic engineering. As the dramatic case of the Dupont mouse illustrates,[12] we now have the capability of modeling genetic diseases in animals by actually inserting the defective gene into the animal. Since many genetic diseases are particularly horrible in that they cause a great deal of suffering, this new technology has the potential for creating enormous amounts of suffering in the laboratory animals created to model the disease. One excellent example is Lesch-Nyhan syndrome, where a defect in uric acid metabolism results in children self-mutilating horribly and experiencing spastic neurological symptoms. The creation of a mouse model for this disease has actually been described. Clearly, such approaches to the study of disease are likely to increase exponentially as the technology develops. The obvious question that arises is how one can control the suffering in such animals. I have seen no discussions of this issue in any journal. There are no specific regulatory apparatuses for such husbandry; yet the issue will clearly soon be upon us. I would urge the research community to consider the care of these animals as a major ethical challenge and adopt a policy of rendering these animals decerebrate, constantly anesthetized, or otherwise rendered incapable of pain, suffering, or other distress.

In this brief discussion, I have attempted to sketch some of the most salient questions, theoretical and practical, that I believe will arise in the near future in the evolution of social concern regarding the use of animals in research. I believe that this evolution will require ever-increasing sophistication in ethical analyses, with the research community having to become far more sensitive to subtle ethical notions and distinctions, and society as a whole and animal advocates in particular having to become far more sophisticated regarding scientific concepts and practices. I believe that society will demand ever-increasing control over what animal research will be funded and that cost benefit will serve as a major measuring rod. I also believe that society will demand environments for animals used in research—and indeed for all animals in our hands—that allow the animals to live happily. Finally, I see genetically engineered animals created to model human disease as an area in need of immediate concern and reflection if the research community is to respect the ever-increasing social concern for the happiness and well-being of laboratory animals.

NOTES

1. W. T. Keeton and J. L. Gould, *Biological Science* (New York: W. W. Norton, 1986), p. 6.

2. S. Mader, *Biology: Evolution, Diversity, and the Environment* (Dubuque, Iowa: W. E. Brown, 1987), p. 15.

3. Michigan State *News* (February 27, 1989): 8.

4. *U. The National College News* (February 27, 1989): 8.

5. J. Katz, "The Regulation of Human Experimentation in the United States—A Personal Odyssey," *IRB* 9, no. 1 (1987): 1–6.

6. B. E. Rollin. "The Frankenstein Thing," in J. W. Evans and A. Hollaender (eds.), *Genetic Engineering of Animals: An Agricultural Perspective* (New York: Plenum, 1986), pp. 285–98.

7. "Universities Fight Animal Activists," *Science* (January 6, 1989): 18.

8. T. Cooper and J. Stucki, "Commentary on Rowan and Rollin," *Perspectives in Biology and Medicine* 27 (1983): 18–21.

9. A. Rowan and B. E. Rollin, "Animal Research, For and Against: A Philosophical, Social, and Historical Perspective," *Perspectives in Biology and Medicine* 27 (1983): 1–17.

10. For detailed discussion, see B. E. Rollin, "Federal Laws and Policies Governing Animal Research: Their History, Nature, and Adequacy," in J. M. Humber and R. F. Almeder (eds.), *Biomedical Ethics Review–1990* (Clifton, N.J.: Humana Press, 1991), pp. 195–229.

11. Dr. Thomas J. Wolfle, personal communication.

12. See U.S. Congress, Office of Technology Assessment, *New Developments in Biotechnology: Patenting Life-Special Report*, OTA-BA-370 (Washington, D.C.: U.S. Government Printing Office, April 1989), p. 99.

Part Five

Beyond Traditional Approaches

16

Scratching the Belly of the Beast

Alan Freeman and Betty Mensch

For the animal should not be measured by man. In a world older and more complete than ours they move finished and complete, gifted with extensions of the senses we have lost or never attained, living by voices we shall never hear. They are not brethren, they are not underlings; they are other nations, caught in with ourselves in the net of life and time, fellow prisoners of the splendor and travail of the earth.

—Henry Beston

The appreciation of the separate realities enjoyed by other organisms is not only no threat to our own reality, but the root of a fundamental joy. . . . [I]t is with this freedom from dogma, I think, that the meaning of the words "celebration of life" becomes clear.

—Barry Lopez

For five years we have been teaching about our relationship with animals and nature. This essay is the product of that enterprise, which was occasioned by our need to sort out a bizarre and contradictory experiential reality—our relationship with our dog, Bruno. For six years we lived as if in bondage to a tall, seventy-pound German short-haired pointer, bred

From *Tikkun* 4, no. 5 (1989): 34–36, 92–94, 95–96. Reprinted with permission of Tikkun, a bimonthly Jewish critique of politics, culture, and society, based in Oakland, California. Subscriptions: $25/yr (six issues). Call (800) 545-9364.

by experts to be the perfect all-purpose hunting dog—sure of foot, keen of scent, willing to brave tangled underbrush and icy waters to retrieve its prey. The real Bruno was neurotic, cowardly, obsessive, and a constant source of household tension. At three months, however, Bruno had been a cute puppy who caught our attention as he stared out from the cramped confinement of a pet-store cage. The next day he was ours, and was to be ours for six long years.

Respectful of Bruno's noble hunting ancestry (although he himself was both gun-shy and afraid to swim), we tried to give him a chance to exert himself in wooded settings. For a time we dragged our one-year-old child out for daily dog walks after work, until Bruno caught and ate a squealing baby badger.

Bruno's enormous physical skills, out of all proportion to his sense, fueled his every move with anxiety-ridden energy. After discovering he could dig holes, for example, he transformed the small but well-landscaped backyard behind our new house into a series of deep, muddy moon craters, which he then stocked with rotting garbage. Our house had come with a fenced-in yard, but, alas, the fence stopped at four feet, which Bruno learned to take in a single bound. Within days the police arrived to tell us that "the big gray dog" had been spotted by neighbors down the street destroying their garden.

In a state of humiliation for our unneighborly behavior, we spent more than $2,000 in landscaping and fence expenses. And Bruno later managed to gore himself leaping the new pointed wood fence, leading to $800 in vet bills, along with thrice-weekly trips to the vet for most of a summer to have his surgical wounds drained.

These anecdotes merely skim the surface of Bruno reality. They leave out the fact that our six-year-old lived in constant fear during his first three years, sure that Bruno would eat him, for Bruno regularly wolfed down anything he could seize from the poor child's high-chair tray. And nothing can capture the experience of awakening to Bruno's loud whining at four in the morning, assuming he really had to go, and then discovering he just wanted to watch for the rabbit on the other side of the fence. On one such occasion, Alan punched him in the mouth, learning through extreme knuckle pain that one *never* punches a dog in the mouth.

In Buffalo, New York, where we live, more than half the children in the public schools live in poverty. Yet we spent enormous sums to maintain and accommodate Bruno. At any time we could have asked the vet to "put him to sleep," as the euphemism goes, and as the vet quite frankly suggested. But we felt we had made a commitment to Bruno. He was a fellow being whom we had taken into our home, and we experienced him as such, not just as a toy to be discarded should it cease to be amusing.

The bottom line is contradiction. Our experience of Bruno was utterly at odds with deliberate, rational analysis of our situation. In this respect, we soon discovered, we were not alone. In American culture at large, treatment of pets is riddled with contradiction. We spend $8 billion per year keeping dogs and cats, often in absurd luxury (grooming parlors, jewelry, even fur coats for some). Pet food takes up more supermarket shelf space than any other commodity, even though the proliferation of advertised flavors and textures does nothing to benefit animal health. What we don't wish to know, however, is how many animals suffer and die as a direct result of our pet-keeping practices. Of the 72,000 dogs and cats born daily in the United States, only one in five finds a home. Shelters destroy some eighteen million unwanted animals each year, while other unwanted pets live short miserable lives scrounging for food: major cities like New York and Los Angeles have about 100,000 wild dogs each.

We abhor the eating of dogs or cats as akin to cannibalism. Shelters therefore refuse to export cat and dog bodies for use as human food, fearing public outcry, yet these same discarded bodies are regularly sent to rendering plants to be recycled into low-phosphate detergent and hog and chicken food, a practice that seems to pass as minimally acceptable.

Our culture tolerates those who lavish affection and resources on pets, but when totemistic affection is expressed through bestiality, we find the behavior despicable. Pet keeping has been called a form of petty domination, with its origins in decadent aristocratic traditions—perhaps a way of mediating our contradictory attitudes toward incest taboos, given the limited license pets provide to fondle warm, furry bodies within a familial setting. Nevertheless, these put-downs do not capture the almost magical contact that occurs when, for example, dogs are used to help emotionally disturbed children regain their connection to the world. What is the meaning of that dog-person bond? It is not universal, for the treatment of pets is as various as the cultures of the world. In some areas, dogs have traditionally been regarded as scavengers and "pestiferous vermin." This is still the case in Northern Thailand, where dogs keep the compounds clean in the absence of bathrooms. There, to eat dog is considered revolting because dogs are low creatures who eat feces. On the other hand, the West has no monopoly on affection for dogs. Early explorers in Australia found that Aborigine women nursed dingo pups along with their own infants, and the pups were lovingly raised in the household.

Our own culture's paradoxical and contradictory relationship with pets is but a subset of our relationship with animals generally. We simultaneously know and do not wish to know the truth. Animal suffering makes us anxious and uncomfortable, yet most of us want to make "rational" use of animals for our own well-being. Think about calves confined in crates in darkness, so starved for iron that they drink their own urine, so starved for maternal affection that they suck desperately at any object offered them; or caged laboratory rabbits whose eyes are doused with burning, blinding chemicals.

Eager to experience haute cuisine without cholesterol, many of us happily devour veal dishes despite the bleak, anguished experience of the calves whose flesh, we know, supplies the meat. And we regularly anoint our selves with perfumes, powders, sprays, and ointments to enhance our capacity to attract other human animals, employing for the purpose cosmetics tested by tormenting hapless creatures.

Although we often choose to ignore animal reality, few topics grip public attention with the force of an animal story. The single biggest media event during the 1988 presidential campaign was the dramatically depicted plight of some stranded whales off the Alaskan coast. The most sophisticated manipulators of our consumer consciousness, those who design ads for beer, know that nothing sells their product so well as dogs (or perhaps the combination of dogs and sex, which is even more curious). And our children's books are filled with furry, warm, loving animals, whom our kids relate to as fellow beings, at least until they sit down to dine on some of them.

Animal rights activists, usually dismissed by intellectuals as bourgeois sentimentalists, have recently gained surprising political clout. *Newsweek* reported in May 1988 that Congress had received more mail on the subject of animal research than on any other topic, and some university experiments have been halted as a result of public pressure. In December George Bush, embarrassed by negative coverage of his annual winter quail-hunting pageant, felt obliged to assure the people, when he later went deep-sea fishing, that he did not hurt the fish; he planned to throw them back into the ocean after catching them.

As environmental disasters (like the Alaskan oil spill, with its attendant animal suffering) multiply, even mainstream voices are recognizing that we cannot simply go on taking the natural world for granted. Today, however, we are not even close to developing an ethically coherent position on the treatment of the environment in general or of animals in particular. Ostensibly straightforward issues prove confounding. For example, the Endangered Species Act, reflecting a kind of Noah's Ark mentality, is clearly premised on the view that some economic sacrifice may be required to preserve the last members of species threatened with extinction. But the act fails to address the fact that extinction usually results from habitat alteration. Preserving habitats is expensive, as has been the case with the vast and uncontaminated territories required by California condors or the "old-growth" forests needed by snowy owls. Suddenly our commitment to preservation becomes a commitment to "rescue" a few last survivors and place them in zoos where, we hope, they will breed. But is a condor outside its habitat really a condor, or simply an artifact preserved by people to assuage human guilt? Moreover, on exactly what basis do we give such special emphasis to the category "species," which is, after all, a human creation, manipulable in its plasticity, as interpreters of the Endangered Species Act have discovered? On what basis does a snail darter have a greater claim to our concern than a raccoon suffering in a trap or a rabbit bred to suffer in a lab?

Even when we make a commitment to preserving a natural habitat, what do we mean by "natural" in a world so changed and dominated by humans? Are fires in Yellowstone "natural"? Wild horses on the western prairies? The hunting of overpopulated deer herds?

We simply lack a vocabulary for analyzing these issues, which are ultimately ethical and theological, not just factual. In the context of human suffering caused by AIDS, the absolutism of those who oppose all animal experimentation seems callous in its indifference; yet the tremendous amount of animal suffering that we impose for trivial purposes (the testing of each new color of cosmetics, for example) may be a sign of spiritual debasement. Opponents of animal rights activists charge them with caring only about animals and having no compassion for people. These opponents remind us that Himmler was a proponent of animal rights, that Hitler was a vegetarian.

Perhaps some modern vegetarians, in their purist zeal, seek to construct a fantasy world for themselves, denying that life is rooted in suffering and death, that we are all, in the end, mere flesh. On the other hand, do we really "need" perfectly tender white veal meat, given the dismal suffering that is the price of its production? Does our insatiable desire for McDonald's hamburgers justify turning tropical rain forests into cattle-grazing pastures? At some point, does not our zeal to make productive use of nature threaten not only the future of the world's ecology, but also our own moral well-being?

If we are to take seriously the suffering and survival of animals, we must at some point confront and reject some basic presumptions of what we have inherited as secular Western Culture. These presumptions are rooted in the social moves we deploy to rationalize hierarchy and domination. These basic moves are to universalize one's particularity, to project its absence onto everyone else, and then to privilege the now-universalized trait as the basis for hierarchical superiority for oneself and reductionist objectification of the Other. Through this process, dominant groups invent names for characteristics of themselves so as to celebrate their own possession of them and decry their absence in others. So named, these traits become images that take on lives of their own: the traits are implicitly universalized, and others are measured by their distance from norms now taken to be objective or natural. Thus has Western Culture identified itself as the triumph of civilization and instrumental rationality.

The English rationalized their brutal oppression of the Irish on the grounds that the latter were "heathen" and "savage," by which the English meant that the Irish were not *English,* which, by definition, meant "Christian" and "civil." Similarly, Africans were categorized as *not white,* and therefore lacking the package of cultural traits associated with whiteness. And men, having defined themselves as the embodiment of rational discourse and moral capacity, have found women by definition lacking in these traits, which means they must play dependent roles. An extreme example of absence-projection is the Freudian notion of penis envy, which, one might suggest, grew out of Freud's inability, in a cultural context of male domination, to imagine himself as a person without one.

In short, over a period of more than three hundred years a particular form of discourse, largely belonging to privileged white men, has claimed for itself the status of Universal Reason. That discourse, which may be characterized as dualistic, analytic, instrumental rationality, has become the yardstick of human hierarchy and privilege in our culture. It also has become the basis for reconceptualizing our relationship to animals and nature so as to rationalize our exploitation and domination of them.

The Western move with respect to nature has been to universalize our particular conception of rationality and then to project its absence onto the rest of creation. We define ourselves as instrumental rationalists, and on that basis we consider ourselves both different from and hierarchically superior to the rest of nature, entitled to use natural resources for our own instrumental ends.

The most rigorous justification for arrogant instrumentalism is rooted in the Western tradition of science, particularly the Baconian view of nature as an unruly force to be dominated and controlled. Often using imagery depicting man as the aggressive scientific inquirer and nature as a woman to be subdued and exploited, Bacon asserted that one could acquire true knowledge about some aspect of nature only by transforming it into an isolated, manipulable object of human scrutiny, something to be prodded and dissected in a strictly controlled laboratory setting. This approach stands in stark contrast to the aspect of traditional, Aristotelian science that calls for observation immersed in natural context as the way to comprehend, in its totality, the essential nature of that which is observed.

The philosophical premises upon which Baconian science rests were enunciated by Descartes, with his strict dualisms of mind/matter and subject (observer)/object (observed). Within this dualistic structure, animals are relegated to the status of mere matter. They are thereby despiritualized, left without cultures or minds of their own, without thought, intention, or feeling. Like the rest of the natural world, they are readily available for instrumental human study and exploitation. In effect, the Christian presumption that only rational creatures have souls has reappeared in the form of secular rationality. As novelist Milan Kundera sums it up:

> Man is master and proprietor, says Descartes, whereas the beast is merely an automaton, an animate machine, a *machina animata*. When an animal laments, it is not a lament; it is merely the rasp of a poorly functioning mechanism.

More than three hundred years after the deaths of Descartes and Bacon, this legacy pervades the modern psychology lab, where animals, wrenched from anything resembling their natural habitats, are shocked, poked, cajoled, and otherwise "stimulated" by a variety of mechanisms, often diabolical; and students are taught never to confuse the observer and the observed by anthropomorphizing or projecting onto animals thoughts, feelings, or a social life of their own. The crucial premise is still that animals are to be regarded as mechanisms whose behavior, however complex, can be reduced to an aggregate of stimulus-response reactions governed by genetic codes.

The model epitomized by the psychology lab has sought to prove its rigor by aping the physical sciences. Ironically, however, the most rigorou physicists have been conceding the fallibility of two of their most treasure traditional presuppositions. One is the dichotomy of theory and fact, whicl maintains that any given explanatory hypothesis can always be objectivel tested—can either be tentatively confirmed or soundly falsified by contrar evidence. As most sophisticated scientists have conceded, however, data gathering and observation are always informed and constrained by pre vailing theoretical paradigms. The strict dichotomy breaks down.

So too with the dualism of subject and object. Starting with quan- tum mechanics and Heisenberg's Uncertainty Principle, and continuing with philosophical counterparts such as Wittgenstein's *On Certainty*, we have come to recognize that reality makes itself known and "objective" only through the lens of the particularly situated observer. We see, as it were, always "through a glass, darkly." Instead of detachment, there can be only context.

A revisit to animal labs shows how they in fact provide a vivid ex- ample of the collapse of the observer/observed dualism. As poet, phi- losopher, and dog trainer Vicki Hearne points out, the presuppositions a researcher brings to the lab inevitably affect not simply the interpreta- tion of what takes place, but also what actually happens. If a dog, who usually starts by trying to be sociable, meets with no response from the behaviorist researcher—who has been taught that animals are incapable of belief, intent, or meaning—then the dog's own capacities will be dead- ened and it will act as robotic as the researcher believes it to be. Since 1895, white rats have been bred specifically for laboratory use. More doc- ile than their wild counterparts, displaying far less social behavior, and given no opportunity to develop skills necessary for life in the wild, the lab rats are, in effect, objects created expressly to meet the needs of "sci- entific" observers—a peculiarly artificial starting point for understanding animal behavior. Cats, by way of contrast, are difficult to "observe" because they will sometimes refuse to perform tasks they have already learned, preferring even starvation to the degradation of compliance with human demands. This extraordinary fact has never been analyzed by behaviorists, who have no available explanatory vocabulary. Determined to Do Sci- ence rather than really understand animals, one venerable professor told a young researcher, "Don't use cats, they'll screw up your data."

Now that this rigid dichotomy separating humans from nature has started to break down, both scientists and philosophers have discovered that animals begin to *look* different: we perceive creatures unlike those we previously regarded as objectified otherness. By paying close attention, we "discover" a new animal reality. Dramatic breakthroughs have occurred in two areas: interspecies communication and the study of animal social life as "culture."

No trait has been so relentlessly universalized to privilege us in the animal kingdom as our capacity to communciate through language. Even if we don't challenge the criterion of superiority, we must recognize that experiments in interspecies communication have shown us that animals are capable of mastering language—despite refutations by behaviorists reminiscent of the Church's response to Galileo. When chimps and gorillas learned to use sign language, there was a rush to deny that this behavior went beyond mere "conditioned association." It is now clear, however, that apes can use symbols to represent things not present, and can generalize concepts (like the chimp Washoe, who learned to sign "open" for a door, and quickly made the same request for drawers, jars, and even faucets).

Facing the loss of their monopoly on "language," recalcitrant humans retreated behind the bastion of "syntax" to describe specifically human, and therefore privileged, linguistic capacity. While the debate goes on (apes may be hesitant in their syntactical ability; dolphins may be quite adept), it is clear that the former bright line between language and "nonlanguage" now eludes us: when Koko the Gorilla picks up a rubber tube and uses it as a straw for drinking while joking in signs about being an "elephant gorilla," or when Michael, now a captive gorilla, sadly describes how "bad men" came and hit his mother on the head so that blood appeared, then the syntax debate begins to look like nothing more than defensive academic quibbling.

While displays of formal linguistic skill have compelled us to recon sider assumptions about animal capacity, there is a sense in which these grammar/syntax/concept debates are simply beside the point. People have, for thousands of years, entered into complex relationships with animals, despite the absence of symbols and alphabets. The stories successful trainers tell of their horses and dogs have a moral dimension totally missing in behaviorist accounts. Implicit and explicit in the trainers' language is the notion that their animals have not only intelligence, but a complex and delicate capacity for moral understanding. When trainers start with the assumption that animals can have a responsible relationship with humans, and when they insist through discipline that the animals act accordingly, they can elicit an extraordinary degree of responsiveness, and what can rightly be called integrity. (Behaviorists, in contrast, make lousy trainers.) This reciprocal trust and shared sense of moral responsibility may constitute the real meaning of "language" between humans and animals.

While our growing awareness of animal communicative skill serves to dislodge us from hierarchical complacency, we persist in measuring animals by their distance from our still-universalized criteria of competence and moral superiority. Much more destabilizing are studies that are starting to show the rich depth of animal life in the wild. There are, it turns out, animal societies all around us about which we know almost nothing. Animals can be conscious and communicative in their own way, not ours; they can have cultures of their own, rather than just learning to participate in our culture.

In one of the great flip-arounds in the history of science, it is now argued that animals with the smallest brains are the ones who most require the capacity for conscious thought, since they are least able to contain the complex genetic material necessary to sustain a largely automatic response system. Thus the complex lives of insects have taken on new significance. One of the most successful animals in the world, for example, is the leaf-cutter ant, who performs a wide variety of tasks, including the tending of fungus gardens, while another type of ant is known to "farm" other insect species, feeding, protecting, and even building shelters for its domesticated livestock. So too, the honeybee's "waggle dance" has been called the "second most complex language we know," involving a highly stylized map of landmarks, direction, solar position, and information about the relative desirability of located substances.

Meanwhile, researchers studying mammals with highly developed social structures are starting to write in a manner more reminiscent of sensitive cultural anthropology, again destabilizing our privileged position as bearers of "culture." Their studies have brought about such a blurring of disciplinary borderlines that books about baboons, chimps, and gorillas are often shelved in the anthropology section of bookstores. The pioneer researchers, of course, were Jane Goodall and Dian Fossey; yet in some sense their chimps and gorillas were the easier cases, animals known to be evolutionarily similar to us, to be mysteriously "us" and "not us" at the same time, so that the complexity of their social lives was not altogether surprising.

Those of us who are willing to look are now finding culture in the lives of our more distant cousins in the animal world. Elephants, for example, communicate in ways we are only starting to comprehend—not just through touching and audible trumpeting, but also through infrasonic (low-frequency) calls that carry vast distances, and by way of pheromones and vomeronasal organs, a type of perception for which we have no descriptive word even though it is characteristic of many animal species.

Elephants have a complex social structure, with female-bonded groups at the center and a multi-tiered network of relationships radiating out from them, encompassing the whole population of an area. Ritualized greeting ceremonies express and cement bonds, and vary depending on relationship and length of separation. If a close family group is separated and then reunited, the greetings will be intense and excited—the elephants will run together, rumble, trumpet, scream, click tusks together, entwine trunks, flap ears, urinate, and defecate.

There is no single uniform "elephant": a matriarch who is irritable and tends to go off on her own is unlikely to maintain a closely knit group, but when bonding is close, family affection is intense. Consider the following report by Cynthia Moss, describing what happened when poachers shot Tina, a member of an elephant group Moss had been studying:

The other elephants crowded around, reaching for her. Her knees started to buckle and she began to go down, but Teresia got on one side of her and Trista on the other and they both leaned in and held her up. [Soon, however,] blood gushed from her mouth and with a shudder she died.

Teresia and Trista became frantic and knelt down and tried to lift her up . . . and Tallulah even went off and collected a trunkful of grass and tried to stuff it into her mouth. Finally, Teresia . . . straining with all her strength . . . began to lift her. When she got to a standing position with the full weight of Tina's head and front quarters on her tusks, there was a sharp cracking sound and Teresia dropped the carcass as her right tusk fell to the ground. She had broken it a few inches from the lip well into the nerve cavity. . . .

They gave up then but did not leave. They stood around Tina's carcass, touching it gently with their trunks and feet. Because it was rocky and the ground was wet, there was no loose dirt; but they tried to dig into it with their feet and trunks and when they managed to get a little earth up they sprinkled it over the body. Trista, Tia, and some of the others went off and broke branches from the surrounding low bushes and brought them back and placed them on the carcass. They remained very alert to the sounds around them and kept smelling to the west, but they would not leave Tina. By nightfall they had nearly buried her with branches and earth. They then stood vigil over her for most of the night and only as dawn was approaching did they reluctantly begin to walk away, heading back toward the safety of the park. Teresia was the last to leave. The others had crossed to the ridge and stopped and rumbled gently. Teresia stood facing them with her back to her daughter. She reached behind her and gently felt the carcass with her hind foot repeatedly. The others rumbled again and very slowly, touching the tip of her trunk to her broken tusk, Teresia moved off to join them.

To see such animals as a "different culture" seems directly in accord with the similar deprivileging move going on in contemporary anthropology. Traditionally anthropologists shied away from an emphasis on cultural particularity, fearing excessive contextuality, cultural relativism, and the absence of fixed boundaries. They chose instead to take refuge in analytic categories ("bloodless universals"), such as religion, marriage, property, or trade, which were explicitly or implicitly applied with reference to Western norms. More recently, anthropologists have been recognizing that culture is local, plastic, and utterly particular, best understood not through abstract analytic constructs but through a process that Clifford Geertz calls "thick description." This approach necessarily leads to the rejection of standard hierarchical orderings: for example, Western "civilized culture" contrasted with "primitive culture." Thus recovery of context has a leveling effect. It means that we are all "natives" now; the world must be seen as a place where, in the words of Michael Ignatieff, "difference has its home."

The recovery of context also means that the problem of anthropology (or ethology, or environmental ethics) is the problem of perception. How do we know the other? To deprivilege the claim that our instrumental rationality is the sole path to knowledge serves to underscore the variousness of perception itself: variety in the world is not just variety of "things out there" but variety of perceptual experience, of consciousness itself. Bees, for example, are structured so that they see broken surfaces and movement more easily than we; but they see stationary surfaces less well, and they see colors differently. What to us is a simple white flower is, to a bee, a light blue flower with shimmering, brilliant ultraviolet lines (nectar guides) pointing to the interior. Similarly, "What is it like to be a bat?" has now been posed as a serious philosophical question. Bats perceive the world through sonar: they correlate outgoing, high-frequency, subtly modulated shrieks with subsequent echoes. We can try to imagine hearing by sonar. We can also imagine, perhaps, having webbing on our arms, or flying about catching insects, or spending days lazily hanging upside down. Yet, at best, that would tell us what it would be like for one of *us* to be a bat, not what it is like for a *bat* to be a bat.

That we lack the words for a true phenomenology of bat experience is hardly surprising, since we also lack the words for a true phenomenology of the varieties of human experience. We know a great deal about human beings as objects of study; we know very little about how to get access to each other's inner lives. With respect to animals, insensitivity to the problem of perception all too easily distorts our observations. For example, as Barry Lopez points out, the male researchers who have dominated the study of wolves through field investigation have used almost paramilitary language to describe structures of hierarchy in wolf packs (where "lieutenant wolves" are "dispatched" and an individual wolf "pulls rank" on another). It is becoming evident, however, that wolf hierarchies are more fluid, shifting, and complex than once supposed. Similarly, rituals of "dominance" in baboon culture, once perceived in human terms as indicating a rigid hierarchical power structure, have now revealed themselves to be largely the behavior of insecure newcomers to an otherwise stable group. Success in dominance has, in the long run, little to do with access to material benefit.

So too our distorted perception colors our view of animal territoriality. Just as libertarian apologists for capitalism find Lockean property rights in any tribal culture that has a relationship with its things, wolf researchers have tended to see in "territory" something resembling our ownership of land, or even the boundaries between nation-states. For wolves, however, the importance of territory, the boundaries of which are not fixed but shifting, seems to lie in its relation to pack communication through scent marks. Scent marks within an area provide a cognitive map for wolves, a sense of spatial organization; for by smell a wolf can tell where others in the pack have hunted successfully, or where they have traveled recently.

A somewhat different anthropomorphic tendency is to reject the mechanistic sterility of behaviorism only to adopt celebratory romanticism. We do wolves a great disservice when we describe them as embodying the true nobility we would like to find more often in human society, while we wish away aspects of wolf life that offend our liberal sensibilities. Wolves sometimes kill other wolves. They also kill young members of prey herds, not just the old and sick, with the choice of victim depending on a complex interplay of signals we cannot yet decipher. Despite the myths of environmentalists, wolves sometimes kill beyond their needs, and probably have killed unarmed people during periods of leanness, when taking human prey was worth the risk. The process of hunting is not especially attractive, for wolves run their prey to the point of bloody exhaustion, ripping at the flanks and abdomen, tearing at the nose and head. When the prey is lying on the ground, the wolves will bite open the abdominal cavity and start eating, sometimes before the animal is dead.

Romanticism carries risks far graver than an occasional pretty fantasy about the natural nobility of animals. The grotesque racism of the Nazis was part of a more general ideology that celebrated a spiritualized conception of nature. Early versions of Nazi anti-Semitism were based specifically on the fact that Jews, as city dwellers, had never been part of the rural German *Volk* tradition of closeness to natural forces. Early nazism represented a rejection of academic scientific rationalism, along with modern technology, and a quest for a more authentic spiritual connection to the natural world. In its most virulent form this ideology became the romanticization of precisely those aspects of nature with which liberals are least comfortable—nature's inexorable indifference to individual suffering, the genetic elimination of the least fit in favor of the strongest, and the seeming irrelevance of the "self" in the grand natural order of things.

The Germans, who in Germany today are trying to fashion a politics rooted in a more sensitive concern for the environment, are themselves plagued by the shadow of nazism. The challenge is to understand nature from a more ethically sensitive perspective than instrumental rationality offers, yet to do so without falling into the trap of romanticism. That challenge, in turn, has everything to do with the limits and possibilities of perception.

Other cultures may at least offer some guidance. With respect to wolves, for example, many Western scientists who, rightly, want to really *know* about wolves, to know their reality rather than some romantic image of them, go about their task with a peculiarly aggressive spirit, as if with enough radio collars and microscopes one could bind up the wolf in great lengths of statistical data. While much of that data is useful and informative, Western scientists still know less about wolves than do the Nunamiut people, who, living a hundred miles north of the Arctic Circle, share their lives with wolves. Both the Nunamiut and the wolves must depend on similar hunting techniques to survive, and both have learned to perceive the world in the same way, noting details and making sensory discriminations that would completely elude a Westerner. The Nunamiut, in other words, live in the same "time space" as wolves, and it is different from ours.

Although the Nunamiut's knowledge of wolves, as related by Barry Lopez, is much more detailed than ours, it is not complete; for Nunamiuts there is no single ultimate wolf reality, which is "not a thing to be anxious over." Thus the Eskimo's knowledge of wolves tends to be open-ended, having to do with variation and possibility rather than certainty, particularity rather than universality. Eskimos speak more often of individual wolves than a collective "wolf":

> *Amaguk* [Wolf] may be a wolf with a family who hunts with more determination than a yearling wolf who has no family to feed. He may be an old wolf alone on the tundra, tossing a piece of caribou hide up in the air and running to catch it. He may be an ill-tempered wolf who always tries to kill trespassing wolves wandering in his territory. Or he may be a wolf who toys with a red-backed mouse in the morning and kills a moose in the afternoon.

Native Americans in general did not traditionally consider themselves apart from nature in the way we do; but that does not mean they refused to perceive difference. To perceive difference was not to constitute hierarchy. Just as there were "the People," so too were there "the Bears," "the Mice" and so forth. Animals were simply separate nations, each with particular qualities from which one could learn by paying respectful attention.

In contrast, given our entrenched ideologies, it is hard for us simply to *see* both similarity and differences without rushing to rankings and dualistic categories. The hold of conventional categories is so extraordinary that even Peter Singer and Tom Regan, two of the English-speaking scholars most visibly committed to animal rights advocacy, have argued wholly by reference to Western structures of analytic rationality—Benthamite utilitarianism and deontological libertarianism—as if a new formulation of cost-benefit analysis or a new clarification of Kantian membership criteria will solve what is ultimately a problem in the very nature of our perception. Perhaps for that reason it has been noted that the animal rights movement, with its individualistic emphasis, may be irrelevant, or counter to, a sound environmental ethics.

A first step toward formulating a more sensitive (even sensible) ethics must be, instead, a recovery of humility. We must disabuse ourselves of the cultural version of what Stephen Hawking has called the "strong anthropic principle"—the notion that we are so special that everything else must have assembled itself for the sake of producing us. In the case of other human cultures, our presumption has led to the obliteration of their difference. In 1938, when outsiders had their "first contact" with the fifty thousand previously unknown Papuans of western New Guinea, they discovered literally hundreds of separate cultures, each with its own language. Today anthropologists know of virtually no other human culture, anywhere on earth, that has been untouched by the industrialized West. The point here is not to romanticize any particular lost culture—some practiced self-mutilation, others cannibalism, others child abuse—but rather to recall that the dominant cultures triumphed in their evolutionary short-run for economic and military reasons, hardly qualities that readily correlate with virtue, happiness, or even long-term human survival.

The move toward humility, however, which comes with a renewed appreciation of difference, does not imply that we can solve ethical problems simply by recourse to some essentialist conception of "the natural." This tempting ploy has characterized approaches as diverse as the medieval Scholastic's quest for natural law and the modern sentimentalist's seeking of truth through naturalistic "feel-good" spirituality, the latter approach based on not much more than grooving on selectively chosen experiences of nature at its most pleasurable. In its extraordinary richness of particularity, nature itself yields no morality. Defying the once-common efforts of the pious to find homiletic lessons in every detail of natural life, the world has, as modern theology states, "come of age" in secular times, which may be science's greatest gift to faith. Out there, beyond our limited perceptual capacities, nature is what it is—unrelentingly objective, and unbounded and unexplained by our human moral preoccupations.

To emphasize perceptual distance is not to suggest that we stand uniquely *outside of nature,* but, rather, to remind ourselves that we are bound by what Hawking has called the "weak anthropic" principle—that "we see the universe the way it is because we exist." We are animals who regularly mythologize the finitude of mortality, who seek God and try to discover in our dialectical engagement with the universe the meaning of our own compassion. As such, we can neither abdicate responsibility nor return to the hubristic illusion that we can fashion a unitive, trans-natural morality. God sends us back to the world as it is (however provisional its reality), and to us as we are.

We can therefore offer little solace to those who demand prescriptive norms. We cannot tell you, for example, that you must be vegetarians, that all animal experimentation must cease, or even that we followed the path of moral correctness with respect to Bruno, who, finally, met with good fortune. (A teenage friend took Bruno to to live with him when he left home to go to college. Bruno now resides in the country and we have told our small children that Bruno went away to college.) There is, to be sure, a trendy tendency to fashion environmentally appropriate ethical norms and systems by taking a largely preconceived agenda (for example, nature preservation or vegetarianism) and shoring it up with an eclectic appeal, in the manner of legal argument, to various bits of Scripture, "Eastern" religion, Native American legend, philosophy, and congenial scientific data. It is as if, faced with the environmental disaster we have created, we now seek the comfortable assurance that God is, after all, a committed environmentalist. We forget that God cannot be confined by our human need for an ally. As Dietrich Bonhoeffer wrote, "The only God who can help us is the one who cannot help."

To reject this trendy eclecticism is not to suggest that we wallow in relativism, but to urge that we must recover a more serious theological process, one rooted in context. The recovery of context is thus a part of the true agenda of "postmodernism"—a theological agenda rather than a decadent self-indulgent aesthetic affectation. Just as conventional religion was compelled to confront the seeming triumph of scientific, positivistic secularism to the point of virtually conceding the "Death of God," so too the perceptual changes wrought by the collapse of that secular worldview demand a theological response. This is to suggest neither a misguided "fundamentalism" that tries to recover a prescientific mode of being nor a retreat to a premodern romanticized view of nature. We need a theological practice that is contextual, dynamic, and just as responsive to the fall of secularism as it was to its rise.

As Jews, we will surely wish to reflect, for example, on the humbling unity of living creatures who are, after all, *kol basar* (all flesh), each infused with *ruakh khayyim* (spirit of life). Why did God promise us a covenant (*berit*) with "the beasts of the field and with the fowls of heaven and with the creeping things of the ground" (Hosea 2: 20)? As Christians, we may wonder why it is that Christ, rejecting all preconception, appears where least anticipated. He is present in the least among us, the most marginalized, the "stranger" and the "other," always in their unexpected, irreducible particularity. What then is the meaning of the injunction to "love thy neighbor"?

To speak in such starkly sectarian terms is to affirm the necessarily pluralistic character of the modern theological agenda. We cannot leap to essentialist universals about "life" that deny and mask the rich particularity of living experience and of human tradition. Nor can we retreat into defensive sectarian insularity. As we allow ourselves to confront the particularities of penguins and wolves, grasshoppers and crows, we may discover the basis for a postmodern pluralism, not of nihilistic despair, but of transformative renewal.

Selected Bibliography

Clark, Stephen. *The Moral Status of Animals*. New York: Oxford University Press, 1984.

Dawkins, Marian Stamp. *Animal Suffering: The Science of Animal Welfare*. London: Chapman and Hall, 1980.

Fox, Michael Allen. *The Case for Animal Experimentation*. Berkeley, Calif.: University of California Press, 1986.

Frey, R. G. *Interests and Rights: The Case Against Animals*. New York: Oxford University Press, 1980.

Harvard University Office of Government and Community Affairs. "The Animal Rights Movement in the United States: Its Composition, Funding Sources, Goals, Strategies, and Potential Impact on Research." Based on research by Phillip W. D. Martin. September 1982.

Linzey, Andrew. *Christianity and the Rights of Animals*. London: Spck, 1987.

Midgley, Mary. *Animals and Why They Matter*. Baltimore, Md.: Penguin Books, 1983.

Regan, Tom. *The Case for Animal Rights*. Berkeley: University of California Press, 1983.

———, ed. *Animal Sacrifices: Religious Perspectives on the Use of Animals in Science*. Philadelphia: Temple University Press, 1986.

Rollin, Bernard E. *Animal Rights and Human Morality*. Buffalo, N. Y.: Prometheus Books, 1981.

Rollin, Bernard E. *The Unheeded Cry: Animal Consciousness, Animal Pain and Science*. New York: Oxford University Press, 1990.

Ryder, Richard. *Victims of Science*. London: David-Poynter, 1975.

Sapontzis, S. F. *Morals, Reason, and Animals*. Philadelphia: Temple University Press, 1987.

Singer, Peter. *Animal Liberation*. New York: Random House, 1975.

———, ed. *In Defence of Animals*. New York: Basil Blackwell, Inc., 1985.

Sperling, Susan. *Animal Liberators: Research and Morality*. Berkeley, Calif.: University of California Press, 1988.

Spiegel, Marjorie. *The Dreaded Comparison: Race and Animal Slavery*. Philadelphia: New Society Publishers, 1988.

Contributors

CARL COHEN, Professor of Philosophy, University of Michigan.

ALAN FREEMAN, Professor of Law, State University of New York at Buffalo School of Law.

J. A. GRAY, Institute of Psychiatry, University of London, London, England.

PETER HARRISON, Tutor in the Department of Religious Studies, University of Queensland, Australia.

EDWIN CONVERSE HETTINGER, Professor of Philosophy, College of Charleston, Charleston, South Carolina.

BETTY MENSCH, Professor of Law, State University; of New York at Buffalo School of Law.

TOM REGAN, Professor of Philosophy, North Carolina State University.

BERNARD E. ROLLIN, Professor of Philosophy, Colorado State University.

RICHARD D. RYDER, Senior Clinical Psychologist, Warneford Hospital, Oxford, England.

RICHARD H. SCHWARZ, President, Associated Medical Schools of New York.

PETER SINGER, Director of the Center for Human Bioethics, Monash University, Clayton, Victoria, Australia.

WILLIAM TIMBERLAKE, Department of Psychology, Indiana University.

MARY ANNE WARREN, Professor of Philosophy, San Francisco State University.

ROBERT B. WHITE, Professor of Psychiatry at the University of Texas Medical Branch, Galveston, Texas.

ROBERT WRIGHT, Senior Editor, *The New Republic*.

STEVEN ZAK, Court Attorney for California in the County of Los Angeles.